LAMBORGHINI

The Legend

N666 LAM

Lamborghini Great Britain Limited (01734) 327560

LAMBORGHINI
The Legend

David Hodges

Page 1: Ferruccio Lamborghini used a charging bull badge on tractors, and later on his cars. Page 2: The Diablo has great presence, and in various forms sustained the company through the 1990s. Page 3: The Jalpa was a modestly successful model in the early 1980s. Page 5: An imposing rear view of a Diablo roadster.

Figures and data in this book are quoted in metric measurements first, with the Imperial equivalents noted in brackets.

© Parragon 1997

This edition published in 1998 by SMITHMARK Publishers, a division of U.S. Media Holdings, Inc., 115 West 18th Street, New York, NY 10011.

SMITHMARK books are available for bulk purchase for sales promotion and premium use. For details write or call the manager of special sales, SMITHMARK Publishers, 115 West 18th Street, New York, NY 10011.

Produced by Parragon
Units 13-17, Avonbridge Trading Estate, Atlantic Road, Avonmouth, Bristol BS11 9QD United Kingdom

ISBN 0-7651-0846-1

Designed and produced by Touchstone

Printed in Italy
10 9 8 7 6 5 4 3 2 1

Photographic credits:

All photographs by **Neill Bruce Motoring Photolibrary**, with the exception of the following:
(Abbreviations: r = right, l = left, t = top, b = below)

The John Bech Archive, Denmark: 11, 22(*b*), 23, 27, 36, 52-53, 55(*t*).

Autocar Archives: 9(*b*), 14, 37, 73(*b*), 75.

David Hodges Collection: 7(*t*), 9(*t*), 10, 13, 18, 25(*r*), 37, 40(*b*), 43(*l*), 48, 58(*t*), 76, 77, 78, 79(*tl*), 79(*b*).

Bengt Ason Holm Collection/Roberto Carrer: 6.

Ital Design: 60, 61(*main picture*), 61(*br*).

Andrew Morland: 3, 7(*b*), 15, 16, 17, 20, 21, 25(*l*), 29(*b*), 30, 31, 32, 33, 40(*t*), 41, 42(*b*), 43(*r*), 51(*t*), 53(*t*), 56-57.

Ferrucio Lamborghini S.p.A. & The Peter Roberts Collection with Neill Bruce: 12, 19(*t*), 24, 29(*t*), 35, 45, 49, 52(*l*), 55(*b*), 59, 72, 73(*t*), 74.

Maurice Rowe: 22(*t*), 50, 51(*b*), 54, 58(*b*).

Neill Bruce and the publishers would like to thank all the owners who have made their cars available for photography, especially the following:

Mike Barker at the **Midland Motor Museum:** BMW M1 and maroon Espada 400GT.

Brooks Auctioneers: Bob Wallace Jarama special.

The Haynes Sparkford Motor Museum: LP400S.

Adrian Walker: 1994 Diablo.

The Earl of March for the wonderful Goodwood Festival of Speed.

Special thanks to Mrs Dani Butters at **Lamborghini S.p.A.**, and Ms Fiona Loader in the **Lamborghini GB** Press Office, for all their help and patience.

Contents

Introduction

LAMBORGHINI is essentially Italian, essentially a manufacturer of inspired supercars. This aura is infinitely more important than mere facts, for the first perception is not wholly accurate . . .

The company was the creation of Ferruccio Lamborghini, an industrialist whose name it perpetuates, although he sold his last interests in it in 1974. From the outset, his venture into automobile manufacture was seen as a challenge to Ferrari, and towards that end he established a green-site factory a few miles from Modena, attracted talented young men, and defined a policy aimed at a range of up-market cars.

Below: The badge on the first 350GTV was complemented by a facsimile signature.

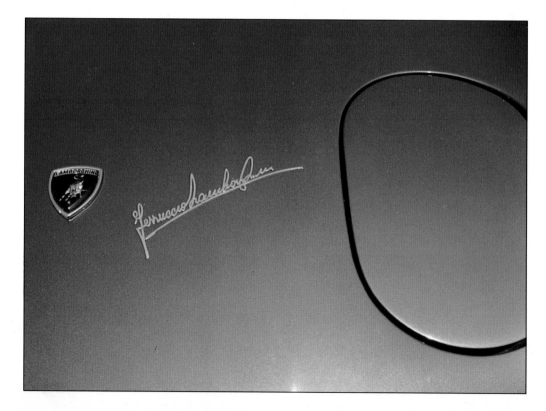

However, his marque soon gained the supercar image that has been simultaneously both a strength, and a sapping weakness. Lamborghini has a very strong presence and has built up a loyal customer following, yet at times its survival has been in doubt, for the supercar market is tiny – the share of it that Lamborghini might have expected at any one time has often been insufficient to sustain the company, the more so as it has not displaced its great Italian rival, in sales or public esteem.

Ferruccio Lamborghini's original intentions were not carried through to create a consistent policy, and that damaged its business when general market conditions turned down. The factory created for the car company was over-size and over-equipped for the one-model supercar ranges that were to come. In that perspective, the dazzling Miura perhaps led to supercar tunnel vision, whereas Lamborghini had always preferred to develop other types in parallel – 'businessman's express' models, for example – and seemingly never liked the mid-engined supercars. In the early years, balanced ranges seemed to be taking shape. But some models lacked flair, or maybe just seemed pedestrian alongside the milestone Miura and Countach supercars. There was promise in the smaller sports/GT cars of the 1970s and 1980s, although this theme was not always followed through logically.

Ferruccio Lamborghini never wavered from his decision not to commit his car company to racing, and as far as pitching a works team into the big time, into competition with Ferrari, was concerned, that was no more than sensible. However, a competitions department or a customer

Above: A purposeful Lamborghini tractor.

car race preparation department could have generated useful business, and a wider sales base.

The early cars, 350GT and 400GT 2+2, were cited as evidence that a racing background is not essential to success as a manufacturer of fine high-performance cars, although this overlooked the careers of Bizzarini and Dallara, for both came from companies which had strong competition histories (Ferrari and Maserati respectively), and their personal inclinations.

Over-generalizing, problems built up after Lamborghini had launched another venture at the end of the 1960s, as if to signal his declining interest in cars, and then bought the farm to which he was

to retreat when he sold his remaining shares in Automobili Ferruccio Lamborghini SpA in 1974. His first Lamborghini team broke up too – designer Giampaolo Dallara, his successor Paolo Stanzani and development engineer Bob Wallace, who was always able to generate much sympathetic coverage for all things Lamborghini among English-writing journalists, all left. The men who followed in the 1970s were worthy, but hardly exciting characters – Franco Baraldini, soon succeeded as chief engineer by Marco Raimondi, and Luigi Capellini, who was briefly general manager. Other moves reflected

company changes, but Ubaldi Sgarzi, who joined the company in 1967 and became its sales manager, served on through all of these changes, into the 1990s, when he was obviously under-impressed by the one-model (Diablo) product line.

Business problems overshadowed personnel changes. Widespread industrial unrest in Italy affected the Lamborghini companies in the late 1960s, when the founder started to distance himself from the concern, and there were particular problems with Lamborghini Trattrice (tractors), which was eventually to be sold to Fiat. The inspired Miura and the fact that sales topped 400 cars for the first time in 1970 made the car company attractive, and a viable means to raise cash, so a controlling interest was sold to Swiss industrialist Georges-Henri Rossetti. Illness meant that he played little part in developing or running the company, although that had been his declared intention. The oil crisis that came in 1973 dealt another blow, and in the following year Lamborghini sold his remaining holding to another Swiss, Rene Leimer. From that point, references to 'Lamborghini' signify the company only, not its founder.

7

Above: The Sant'Agata Bolognese factory in the 1980s.

While Rossetti and Leimer soon moved to sell Lamborghini – Canadian Walter Wolf being courted as a possible buyer – there were promising developments. Baraldini and Capellini brought in new business ideas for a specialist manufacturer, notably leading to the association with BMW in the M1 project and the Cheetah programme with Mobility Technology International.

The BMW M1 was a mid-engined car in road and sports-racing forms, which the German company conceived as a challenge to Porsche. It was to be developed by outside specialists, primarily Lamborghini who were to be responsible for the chassis, while Giugiaro (of Ital Design) was commissioned to style the body. Prototype work was sluggish, as Lamborghini struggled to survive,

and eventually lost the job to Ital Engineering – a company set up by Capellini! Then the Cheetah programme ended prematurely, although this effort was to lead Lamborghini towards its LMs in the 1980s.

Tantalizingly, some felt that the BMW association could have blossomed as a partnership, which could have brought stability to Lamborghini. However, a local court declared Lamborghini bankrupt, and the legal technicalities were such that a government nominee, inevitably an accountant, took on the running of the company. But Dr Alessandro Artese served Lamborghini well during his brief stewardship, approving the Countach development that led to the S model, when production of the original had fallen to 16 units in

1978, and bringing in Giulio Alfieri, formerly technical director of Maserati, to oversee that project and the Jalpa, and to run the plant. A German consortium seemed set to take on the company late in 1979, but negotiations with the Mimran industrial group from 1980 were to prove fruitful (although it was said that Patrick Mimran was the only serious contender at the decisive sale moment in 1981). So Nuova Automobili Ferruccio Lamborghini SpA was established.

The Mimran brothers' ownership lasted until 1987, when the Chrysler Corporation took over – one move in a series of US acquisitions of

Below: Lost opportunity for Lamborghini – BMW M1 as it was eventually marketed, with no Sant'Agata involvement.

Above: The sensational Bertone Countach LP500.

European specialists. One of the first fruits of this development was a four-door Lamborghini, the Portofino concept car. More importantly, Chrysler underwrote Lamborghini Engineering and an entry into Grand Prix racing that was at least partly in the name of Chrysler. That was not an outstanding venture, but from its Modena base, Lamborghini Engineering undertook research for Chrysler and contributed to the Diablo, and then under another new management began to develop projects such as the MegaTech world modular engine (WME) powerplant range. At one stage it was even involved in a racing bob-sleigh project!

A prospectus issued with a Diablo release at Monte Carlo in January 1990 now seems wildly optimistic: 'The Diablo launch closes a period of consolidation and opens one of expansion that will lead to production in excess of 1000 units per year by 1992,'

Chrysler had begun to lose interest in the early 1990s, as losses mounted – the factory was virtually closed for more than three months in 1992. When it did open that year, production ran at a trickle and losses were heavy. The next year was also lean, and rumours of another sale began to circulate. Chrysler let it be known that Lamborghini was available, but not at a knock-down price . . .

There was some surprise when Lamborghini was bought by the Indonesian-controlled MegaTech group late in 1993, for a rumoured £26 million – just a little more than Chrysler had paid for the ailing company in 1987. A leading figure in this was Tommy Suharto, son of the Indonesian premier. Within months, former Lotus Chief Executive Mike Kimberley joined from GM's Malaysian subsidiary, and moved to Sant'Agata as President of Lamborghini. One of his first key appointments was that of ex-Lotus designer Peter Stevens, who was to undertake a similar role at Lamborghini.

At the time, Lamborghini relied solely on the slow-selling Diablo – with sales forecast to be fewer than 250 in 1996 – and while rumours of new models, or at least a re-skinned Diablo, began to circulate, developments take time . . .

A first step was to build another racing base, with the Diablo one-model series in 1996, largely for hobby racers, but a more realistic enterprise than another dabble in the prestige waters of Grands Prix.

Incidentally, Lamborghini's marine V12s have been very successful in power boat racing. Built in capacities from 5.2 litres to 9 litres, these were selling at rates approaching 300 units a year by the second half of the 1980s, after they had powered the winning boats in the 1985-86 European off-shore championships. A decade later (in 1994) Lamborghini gained the World Class 1 Off-shore Championship. And the 7.2 litre marine V12 had proved useful in Lamborghini off-roaders, when customers wanted something more than the LM002's 5.2 litres . . .

9

Above: LMs were unique off-roaders – costly, brutal, effective.

Cars Great Britain Limited, with dedicated facilities at Porsche's British HQ. Such an arrangement would have been inconceivable a quarter of a century earlier . . .

The lure of supercars remained as strong as it had been in those earlier days, although motor industry soothsayers in the mid-1990s predicted that the type as it was then would not survive long into the 21st century. Lamborghini would have been nothing if it had not built supercars, with performance capabilities way beyond most drivers' abilities, on most roads, in most situations. The company attitude was always realistic, roughly on the lines of telling the buyer of a very expensive motor car what he wanted to be told – maybe the car could not quite reach the speed claimed, but if the dials told the owner that it could and had, he would be happy. So Lamborghini's claimed

Above Diablo SV (Sport Veloce) and the SV-R purpose-built racing version. Right: The first Lamborghini car, the 350GTV on a modest stand at the 1963 Turin Motor Show. Franco Scaglione's body lines found few admirers.

While Lamborghini's overall fortunes had been erratic, its representation in important overseas markets had also been inconsistent – in the USA and Britain there was not always a concessionaire, for instance. For many years Portman Garages, then Portman Lamborghini, was the British distributor. The latter ceased trading early in 1992. Portman Concessionaires took its place later in the year. At the end of 1994 Lamborghini Great Britain Limited was formed as an independent company wholly owned by Porsche

Above: Ferruccio Lamborghini in his vineyard.

performance figures have to be read with this proviso in mind, and indeed some of the production figures might also be read with a mental question mark forming . . .

Be that as it may, MegaTech bought a leading supercar manufacturer. Its directly responsible subsidiary M-Power had to face up to a need for massive cash investment if Lamborghini was to achieve more than survival, even if it was to survive at all; if new high-profile models were to be developed and introduced by the end of the century; if the marque was to resume its long-lost position as a natural challenger to Ferrari and its mystique was to be restored.

FERRUCCIO LAMBORGHINI 1916-1993

Ferruccio Lamborghini was born into a farming family at Renazzo, near Cento in the northern Italian province of Emilia-Romagna, and many years later he was to return to the land. His stocky build and tenacity marked him out as a man of the Italian countryside. Make what you wish of his birth under the Zodiac sign of Taurus, the Bull . . .

His early interests were not agricultural, but mechanical, and after a period of self-tuition he attended a technical school in Bologna. During the Second World War he served in the Regia Aeronautica, the Italian Air Force, working in transport sections, and in 1944-46 served under the British military forces in a similar capacity.

He returned to civilian life in his own small garage, converting military vehicles into tractors and tuning small Fiats, the mainstay of most small Italian automotive boutiques. He raced one of his Fiat specials just once, crashing out of the 1948 Mille Miglia.

Developing his tractor business took all his time, and set him on the way to becoming a millionaire (in any currency). From 'bitza' machines, Lamborghini Trattrice moved on to producing original tractors at the end of the 1940s, and to a comprehensive factory. Soon this was almost self-sufficient, making its own engines and transmission units. The tractors carried a charging bull badge.

Other industrial enterprises followed, primarily making central heating and air-conditioning equipment. Then Lamborghini turned to cars. He ran a succession of high-performance cars, and seemingly felt that they all lacked refinement. Legend has it that he tried to complain to Enzo Ferrari personally – as an industrialist of similar status – but was spurned, and that was the point when he decided to build a better car . . .

These cars were often better, and the products of Automobile Ferruccio Lamborghini SpA (later prefixed by Nuova) are covered in this book. Lamborghini initially seemed to make the right moves, for example in picking his lieutenants in this venture and not putting himself in the hands of a bank, but he soon found the going tough. Supercar manufacture in itself was not enough to sustain a sophisticated factory (how many others were to learn that lesson?), and in the early 1970s his other companies could no longer underpin the enterprise. Lamborghini had to sell, at first a controlling interest and then the complete car company. The tractors went to Fiat; the air conditioning company failed.

Ferruccio moved to his estate near Perugia, further south in Italy, and his name began to be associated with the making of wines. He died early in 1993. His viniculture will soon be forgotten; his cars never will be.

Lamborghini 350GT

THE FIRST Lamborghini promised well, but this 350GTV was a show car, and it was not well received. Efforts were redirected to the 350GT. Like so many Lamborghini models that were to follow, this made its debut at a Geneva Motor Show, in 1964. Perspective is added when some of its contemporaries are recalled – Aston Martin DB5, Bristol 408, Chevrolet Corvette, Ferrari 275 and 330, Jaguar E-Type, Jensen CV-8, Maserati 350GT and Mistrale. The impression was that it would match any of these, and more than match some. Most of them looked good, and were real high-performance cars – Lamborghini was entering a challenging market sector.

In this venture, the company's prime asset was a new V12. It was but one part of the whole package, yet more than that as it was to be fundamental to many Lamborghini models. The 131 350GTs that were to be built were by no means incidental, but the story of the engine comes first.

The V12 was designed by Giotto Bizzarrini, who had worked for Alfa Romeo and Ferrari (notably, he was responsible for the 250GTO) before turning freelance, working for Iso as well as Lamborghini. His design for a 1½ litre Formula 1 V12 appealed to Lamborghini, who commissioned a larger road car engine on similar lines. The first was completed in May 1963, and in its first 3.5 litre

form the prototype produced more than 350bhp in initial tests. As an aside, one of the odd rumours of the mid-1960s suggested that Lamborghini had called in Japanese technicians to supervise the project. Some 20 years later, that story resurfaced in an even odder form, as a journalist 'revealed' that Lamborghini had commissioned Honda to design the engine!

An oversquare (77 x 60mm) twin-overhead-camshaft unit, the Lamborghini engine was more advanced than Ferrari's production sohc V12s. It started life as a dry-sump unit, with an aluminium block and iron liners, hemispherical combustion chambers, two valves per cylinder and two chain-driven overhead camshafts per bank. There was a

Below: A 350GTV in original condition – some cars have been fitted with more effective quad headlights from the 400.

seven main bearing crankshaft. Each bank had a Marelli distributor, and rather than fuel injection there were six Weber twin-choke carburettors, which appeared daunting, save that Lamborghini was confident that once they were properly set up, they would not need adjustment outside routine maintenance intervals.

As announced for the 350GTV in the Autumn of 1963, this engine was rated at 360bhp at 8000rpm, but for the production 350GT it was detuned, for Lamborghini wanted a tractable, smooth and lightly stressed road car engine, not a racing unit. In this form it was rated at 270bhp at 6500rpm.

Bizzarrini's commitment ended at this time, and he went on to make a few cars carrying his own name, the first (the Strada) being a version of the Iso Grifo. He left Lamborghini with a marvellous engine.

Above: Touring's convertible 350GTV is a handsome and rare vehicle. The transverse V12 in the first Miura show chassis is in the foreground, at Turin in 1965. Below: The production coupé had generous glass areas. But six exhausts were perhaps a little ostentatious?

350GTV

The first car it was intended to power was not so marvellous, however. It proved to be a show special, built to convince the motoring world that Lamborghini was serious about his entry into high-performance car manufacture. In its specification were some of the sophisticated ingredients he felt necessary if his company was to compete with Ferrari, notably independent suspension all round, by wishbones and coil springs, disc brakes front and rear, ZF steering and a ZF 5-speed gearbox.

The steel tube chassis echoed racing practices, and was clothed in a body that was sleek but not well balanced in conception – it was said that Lamborghini insisted that stylist Franco Scaglione had to take too many of his own ideas into account. There were curving lines and sharp edges, there were retractable headlights, but also some odd details, and the six exhausts projecting under the tail just seemed flashy. Moreover, some of the panels were steel and some were aluminium, and the workmanship was poor.

However much journalists might have been predisposed to praise another Italian high-performance car, reactions when it was unveiled and then exhibited in a corner at the Turin show were mixed (the quad-cam engine, shown separately, was favourably received). Realistically Lamborghini devoted the winter to a redesign, to create a car to be introduced at Geneva in 1964.

The 350GTV was not a runner, and had weight under the bonnet to make it sit properly. Many years later, enthusiast dealer Romano Bernardoni at Bologna squeezed a V12 into the car, and it ran.

350GT

In five months, Giampaolo Dallara redesigned the chassis and Touring reworked the body. The car on the Geneva stand was on a slightly longer wheelbase, and Touring's lightweight body clothed a new square-tube chassis.

The body was more cohesive, and its lines generally softer. It failed to improve on Scaglione's design in only two points, the oval headlights atop the nose that replaced the pop-up lights, and the conventional front-hinged bonnet top (the complete nose and bonnet of the 350GTV were hinged at the front, like several British sports cars of the period).

Slim pillars made for excellent visibility, and the cockpit was larger. The extra space tempted Touring to add a third little seat astride the transmission tunnel, but that oddity was soon abandoned (a chrome inscription on the tail of the Geneva show car read 'Lamborghini 350GT 2+1'). The internal finish was good, with comfortable seats, a typical thin-rimmed three-spoke steering wheel, a better fascia layout than some models that were to follow, and a lot of leather.

Below: A 400GT, with two pairs of headlights. The main changes in this model were in the engine and cabin space.

In common with other details of the car, there were to be minor cockpit changes through production. Beyond that, Touring built two 350GTS convertibles, with the hood folding down into the space where the third seat had been, and Zagato built a '350GTZ' coupé which distinctly echoed some of that coachbuilder's Ferrari bodies.

In the detuned engine, the dry sump was abandoned and the small cost in engine height this caused was offset as side-draught carburettors were adopted. Other changes were aimed at 'civilizing' the engine, or reducing production costs. Lamborghini normally quoted an output of 270bhp, and a consensus of reports suggested a top speed of the order of 240km/h (150mph).

In 1965 a V12 enlarged to 3929cc appeared (the bore was increased to 82mm). It also had a higher compression ratio. The claimed output was 320bhp, with a corresponding torque improvement. To compete with the Ferrari 275GTB, a few late 350GTs were completed with this engine, becoming 400GTs. Some also had Lamborghini's own transmission, and soon the company was to use few proprietary components. Largely to meet US requirements, late cars had two pairs of headlights in place of the oval units. Most of these cars had all-steel bodies, but seemingly three of the 23 400GTs had aluminium bodies. As far as there was a 'normal' 400GT, it was a car capable of around 250km/h (155mph).

The production figures for these first Lamborghinis seem modest, but they were built

Above: The tail area of Touring's body was aesthetically weak.

when Italy was suffering a recession, by a company that had not made cars before, and they served to bed in the Sant'Agata Bolognese factory.

SPECIFICATION	350GT
ENGINE	60 degree V12, dohc, 3465cc
HORSEPOWER	270bhp @ 6500rpm
TRANSMISSION	Manual 5-speed
CHASSIS	Tubular, with steel platform
SUSPENSION	Independent front and rear
BRAKES	Disc
TOP SPEED	Approx 240km/h (150mph)
ACCELERATION	0-100km/h (62mph): 6.8 seconds

Lamborghini 400GT

THE 400GT 2+2 evolved from the 350GT/ 400GT as Lamborghini took the logical step of providing occasional accommodation behind the two front seats. The two rear seats were cramped, but this development made the first-generation Lamborghini a convincing grand touring car, very much the type Ferruccio Lamborghini had set out to build when he established his car company.

Headlights apart, the 400GT 2+2 inherited the good looks of the first cars, its deeper body even improving on them from some angles. It was some 60mm (2.5in) taller as room was created for the rear seat passengers; to the same end, the floor pan was fractionally lower and the rear suspension slightly modified. The 2550mm (100.4in) wheelbase and 1380mm (54.3in) rear track were unchanged. The rear window was smaller, the boot lid larger.

Bodies were all-steel, and weight was increased by some 150kg (330lb). Carrozzeria Touring was close to oblivion, but its build quality was better than some Lamborghini suppliers to come; the last 400GT 2+2 bodies were produced by Marazzi, a company that rose out of the ashes of Touring.

Before Touring went under, incidentally, it built a shapely one-off on a shortened 2+2 chassis. Named Flying Star II for the company's 1930s bodies, this had quasi-estate car lines behind the side doors, where it was elegantly sharp, even if estate car capacity was negligible. The nose was equally eye-catching, and showed what might have been made of the Lamborghini original, for it was a clean wedge with twin headlights in the front of each wing.

The other special body on this chassis was less noteworthy. Dubbed Monza 400, it was a two-seater coupé built to order by Neri e Bonacini, with low lines that aped contemporary Ferraris. That was carried through to detail, such as the engine-air outlets behind the front wheels, which were dummies in this case!

Left: This 400GT was once owned by Beatle Paul McCartney. The cockpit (inset) is very 'traditional', with a thin-rimmed wheel and clear round instruments.

17

Left: A scintillating 400GT 2+2. Its relationship to the earlier models is clear, although no body panels were identical.

The interior of the regular 2+2 was comfortable, and there was little mechanical or airflow noise. The fascia was not ideal, and some of the controls were heavy – Lamborghini shortcomings that would persist. The handling was generally praised, and little changed by the increased weight, while the ride was highly rated. In terms of measured performance, 0-100mph (roughly 0-160km/h) could be achieved in 15.6 seconds, while the top speed was calculated to be 250km/h (155mph), although that seems suspiciously like a manufacturer's nicely rounded figure. Production, 1966-86, reached 224 as the 400GT 2+2 was run alongside other models, and increasingly overshadowed by them.

SPECIFICATION	400 2+2
ENGINE	60 degree V12, dohc, 3929cc
HORSEPOWER	320bhp @ 6500rpm
TRANSMISSION	Manual 5-speed
CHASSIS	Tubular, with steel platform
SUSPENSION	Independent front and rear
BRAKES	Disc
TOP SPEED	Approx 250km/h (155mph)
ACCELERATION	0-100km/h (62mph): 7.1 seconds

Lamborghini Miura

WITH THE P400, Lamborghini became a very special marque. The concept was exceptional, the appearance of the car was sensational, and its performance was outstanding. It was to be named Miura, for a breed of fighting bull.

Key men Giampaolo Dallara and Paolo Stanzani were racing enthusiasts and drew up a design for a road car on mid-1960s racing lines. There were precedents, notably some Ferraris – especially the 250LM – and the Ford GT40, but in its ingenuity and refinement the Miura outclassed them. Ferruccio Lamborghini approved a development programme on the basis of chassis drawings early in 1965, but from the outset he clearly refused to sanction any development that might direct the project towards becoming a circuit car. His staff accepted that while the Miura would be a road car using much mid-1960s racing car technology, it would never be a competitions car. Enthusiasts outside the factory could dream their dreams, and journalists could file speculative stories about a racing programme . . .

The car was first shown as a chassis, complete with engine, at the Turin Motor Show in November 1965. It was built around a mid-mounted engine, behind the cockpit but within the wheelbase. With the V12 this had seemed to pose problems, as a long wheelbase was not acceptable (had the designers been able to look a quarter of a century into the future, they might have seen a possible solution in the '1+2' layout of the McLaren F1). In fact, the V12 was short enough to be turned through 180 degrees and mounted across the chassis.

Fabricated in steel, the chassis was a shallow monocoque centre section, with pressed sub-frames front and rear. There were large sills and a stout central spine, with box-section bulkheads at the front and rear of the main section (defining the cockpit area). Suspension was by double wishbones and coil springs/dampers front and rear, with an anti-roll bar at each end.

The engine position was crucial, and it seems that the idea of a transverse installation came out of a joint brain-storming session. As the V12 was a fairly narrow unit, it fitted within the target wheelbase. Its use in this position called for a new transmission, and this followed Mini lines, with the gearbox beneath the engine, sharing its oil. A central differential made for symmetry, for example in equal-length driveshafts. The exhausts were complicated, as the lack of longitudinal space meant that transverse silencers had to be used.

Left: The Miura chassis at the 1965 Turin Motor Show might have been for exhibition only, but, much more clearly than a running car, it showed the fabricated sheet steel construction, and transverse V12 installation.

Above and right: The Miura was the first Lamborghini to be widely recognized, and is an abiding supercar shape from the 1960s. It is almost timeless, in large part because there was so little that was flamboyant about it, making it a fine example of the stylist's art.

The bodywork fitted tightly around the engine, and although the unstressed tail was rear-hinged, access was good only if it was removed. The nose – bodywork and the angled radiator – was front-hinged. The battery was in the nose, together with the spare wheel (so far back that it partly overlapped the front bulkhead) and fuel tank, which meant that weight distribution changed noticeably as fuel was used, roughly from 45/55 to 43/57.

The Miura was visually seductive, technically clever. This P400SV was a relatively late car in the last series. It retained the feature of louvres above the engine, but the lights and wider wheels set it apart ('gold' wheels were not normal – setting off a red body they recalled contemporary competition Ferraris!). The slatted trailing edge of the door let air through to the engine compartment (right). The reclining lights (far right) did not have the 'eyebrows' of earlier Miuras; radiator air was exhausted through the outlets atop the nose. The engine compartment (below) was tightly packed.

In the four months between the Turin show in 1965 and the all-important Geneva show in the following Spring a body had to be created. As Touring was known to be failing, and a stylist committed to Ferrari would hardly have been acceptable as a potential long-term associate, Bertone got the job. The car that carried the coachbuilder's badge behind its doors was spectacular. Nuccio Bertone gave the job to his young new designer Marcello Gandini, and undoubtedly kept watch over his shoulder as he shaped the lines that were admirably to complement the Miura's startling mechanical specification.

This specification may have dictated the overall proportions of the body, but its pure lines were a fine example of the stylist's art, and proclaimed the car's purpose – that of carrying two people very rapidly. The Miura was low and wide, with a slender nose and high tail, so there was no mistaking the position of the engine. It was not faultless in detail, but then things like gutters above the doors to keep water out of the cockpit as they were opened would have spoiled the smooth upper surface . . .

The full-width air intake under the nose was hardly noticeable, but the two prominent top vents certainly were, as the lines fell away to the nose. The one on the right also housed the fuel filler cap. In the retracted position, the headlights aligned with the bodywork; they were electrically operated, with no covers, but on the first Miuras there were curious little strakes to accentuate the lights, usually referred to as eyebrows although they were below the lights as well as above them.

There was a sharply raked windscreen, and quite small windows in the large doors. Clever use of a contrasting colour below the sill line drew the eye to neat little scoops for cooling air for the rear brakes. The rear edge of each door had intakes which passed air through the pillars, where it was deflected to the filters, thus ensuring a cold air supply to the engine. Engine air found its way out through prominent transverse louvres. Right at the back, the boot was larger than might have been expected, and as it had a conventional boot lid, it could be accessed without lifting the tail section (on the other hand, it did lift with the rear bodywork).

Below: Symbols. A Miura with a Countach line-up at Monaco during a GP meeting (inset), and somebody brought together a badgeless Miura and a bull. . .

The Miura did not have thick sills, so getting in was not difficult. The cockpit was functional, but cramped for a tall driver despite a wheelbase stretch during development which made for a slightly larger footwell. While the seats had thin backs, they were sensibly angled and supportive, but once again a tall driver was penalized, with no alternative to a 'bent knees' position (not comfortable, and making heel-and-toe changes difficult). Driver seat-fitting was offered to customers. Some of the controls were heavy, especially the gear change. Main instruments ahead of the driver were clear, lesser ones on the centre line were angled towards the driver but were not easy to read. Storage space was limited to a little shelf ahead of the passenger, but modest door bins were introduced later.

With one bank of a V12 only inches from the ears, sound as well as heat insulation posed problems. Noise was ever-present when the engine was pulling, to the extent that conversation was not possible inside the cockpit, and could be interrupted outside it, as the exhausts made exciting sounds. However, there was little wind or tyre noise when free-wheeling with the engine ticking over, which indicated aerodynamic efficiency. The heat-insulated bulkhead/firewall was thick, and so was the plastics rear window above it, so the main source of heat tended to be sun shining through the windscreen. Small extractors helped move air, and the windows could be opened for ventilation. Forward visibility was good, three-quarter rear and rear visibility negligible.

Below: Ferruccio Lamborghini was obviously – and justifiably – proud of this Miura.

Development was largely in the hands of Bob Wallace and did not start until after the Geneva announcement, so that almost a year passed before the first cars were delivered. Later in 1967 the first reports were published. These tended to overlook some quality defects, some of which may have arisen from the production processes – while the complex engine/transmission was an in-house product from castings to completion, the chassis was built by a contractor and then passed to Bertone for the aluminium bodies to be added.

The Miura's performance could hardly fail to impress, and almost invariably reports referred to the Miura as a 'racer for the road'. (Ferruccio Lamborghini still had no intention of being caught between the rock of Ferrari and the hard place of Ford in that respect!). Despite the need to compromise, ride and handling were highly rated, so were adhesion, stability and braking. Most found the steering light, but the other controls heavy. To a degree, and understandably, critics may have been dazzled by the car, for it was not faultless. The nose tended to lift at speed, and apparently there was some chassis flex when the car was driven hard; the

Left: The Jota had a lightweight body with aerodynamic improvements, and a tuned V12.

gear change was unsatisfactory, while early customers 'helped' in the development process, and the Miura gained a reputation for unreliability.

But with a claimed 350bhp – in fact, rather less – to propel a well-balanced car with a kerb weight of 1300kg (2866lb) it was quick. The top speed was around 275km/h (171mph). Variations between engines meant that precise speeds only applied to individual cars.

During production the chassis was strengthened; then in 1969 the P400 gave way to the P400S. This had a revised rear suspension and engine modifications to increase claimed power output to 370bhp at 7700rpm. Among cockpit improvements there were electric window lifts and a proper glove box, while optional air conditioning was listed. The oddity of a batch of switches mounted behind the rear view mirror remained.

The P400SV which came in 1971 was a well-developed car. The body was little changed, but appeared more aggressive as wider wheels had to be accommodated; there were detail improvements as the headlight embellishments were deleted, and there were new rear lights. Trim in the cockpit was better, but an all-round improvement in build quality was more significant than the introduction of real leather seats.

The V12 was uprated again, but its extra 15bhp simply offset increased weight and the drag of wider tyres and there was no improvement on the P400S top speed of 277km/h (172mph). Late in the Miura's life, a ZF limited-lip differential was introduced, while meant that engine and transmission could no longer share oil, and so were separated by a partition.

24

SPECIFICATION	MIURA P400S
ENGINE	60 degree V12, dohc, 3929cc
HORSEPOWER	370bhp @ 7700rpm
TRANSMISSION	Manual 5-speed
CHASSIS	Monocoque centre section, front and rear extensions
SUSPENSION	Independent front and rear
BRAKES	Disc
TOP SPEED	277km/h (172mph)
ACCELERATION	0-100km/h (62mph): 6.1 seconds

It would have been difficult to improve on the Miura's lines in the late 1960s or early 1970s. Bertone did essay a Targa-style spider P400 in 1968, and while this succeeded visually, it was followed up only in odd independent conversions (the Bertone car was sold to the International Lead-Zinc Research Organization, and used for publicity with some zinc-coated panels and other components).

The Jota was a one-off derivative, largely Bob

Above: Reported 'destroyed by fire', the Jota was later seen in the Sant'Agata service department.

Wallace's creation, not very pretty but purposeful and obviously aimed at circuit use. It was much lighter than a Miura, and had some 415bhp in a tuned V12. Lamborghini did not object to this experiment, until cash-flow problems dictated that it was sold. It was badly damaged in a fire following an accident. Independent replica Jotas without any of the high-tech features of this car made no impact.

Miura production ended in 1972, with the last cars delivered early in 1973, to be followed by an odd one two years later. Total production was 762 units, plus the two running prototypes. Although sales fell off during the life of the P400SV (150

Above: Bertone's ZN75 Miura roadster, on a P400 basis, first seen in 1968, was attractive but a dead end.

built), some enthusiasts felt that it could have been continued further into the Countach era. As it was, the Miura worked well for the company, although it diverted it away from Ferruccio Lamborghini's policy of building luxurious GT cars, and thus might not have paid dividends in the long term. It sold many, many more than estimated when it was put into production, and it certainly bestowed on Lamborghini the image it still enjoys. And it remains a beautiful car.

Lamborghini Espada

CARROZZERIA Bertone unveiled one of its motor show sensations at the 1967 Geneva event, the Marzal. This dramatic concept car was seen as an approach to a four-seat Lamborghini – it was by no means a production proposition – and it turned out to be a forerunner of the Espada, a genuine four-seater and a distinctive late-1960's supercar.

Designed by Marcello Gandini, the Marzal was rear-engined, with a 2-litre straight six (half of a Lamborghini V12) mounted transversely behind the rear axle line, slanted to keep at least some weight away from the tail. This layout on an adapted Miura chassis with the wheelbase extended by 120mm (4.7in) made room for four seats. One long gull-wing door on each side gave access to front and rear seats. These doors were largely in glass (with just a little opening section in each), there was a glass roof and a typically large and steeply raked windscreen – 'see and be seen' summed up the cabin configuration. Some of the detailing was flashy, but the overall lines were impressive.

The Marzal was a runner, although the weight was assumed to be considerable, and with just 2 litres to propel it, performance would probably not have been impressive. It was active for about a year, then it was retired.

But together with a Gandini-styled Jaguar E-Type, it led to the Espada (a matador's sword), which appeared in 1968. This was powered by the V12, mounted at the front, and there was a steel platform chassis with integral bodywork and square-tube structures fore and aft to mount suspension, engine and gearbox. The suspension was independent all round, by wishbones and coil springs/dampers, with anti-roll bars front and rear. At an early stage, a hydropneumatic self-levelling system for the rear was tried, but rejected. The worm-and-sector

Below: Espada was a four-seat GT car, here in 1972 form.

Above and left: Bertone's extraordinary Marzal concept car inspired the Espada.

steering was necessarily low-geared, for this was a heavy machine (Ferruccio Lamborghini apparently did not approve of power steering).

This was a wide and bulky car, but Gandini made it look slender from most angles. The broad flat bonnet, the only major body item fabricated in aluminium, fitted tightly onto the V12, which filled the engine compartment. Its surface was broken by two NACA ducts, for the cabin ventilation system. Engine air was taken in through the nose, and exhausted through slots on the sides. Twin lights neatly flanked the plain grille.

The large conventional doors which took the place of the Marzal gull wings gave reasonable access to the rear seats, and side windows were adequate (the small rear pair were top-hinged). In general visibility was better than for most 'supercars' of the period. The tail treatment was clever, for in addition to the large sloping glass tailgate, there was a full-width vertical glass panel right at the back, which made for easy reversing (a manoeuvre some supercar stylists forget). The battery and the spare wheel were below the luggage deck, which was quite large, although it was shallow, so that the load was restricted. The fitted suitcases that were available

were thus a sensible extra. Small grilles behind the side windows concealed the fillers for two interconnected fuel tanks, one in each wing. These had a combined capacity of 90 litres (20 gallons) – none too generous for a car with a fuel consumption of the order of 25 litres/100km, or 11.5mpg, when it was driven hard.

The cockpit gave an impression of luxury that was wholly appropriate, with walnut trim and generous use of leather. The four seats were comfortable, and all had built-in headrests, but leg room in the rear was restricted. A large centre console divided the interior – it was so large that

one might have suspected a backbone chassis, and it did increase chassis strength as well as carrying ventilation ducts.

On the down side, few testers found the driving position acceptable, although Lamborghini claimed that it could be tailored to suit any driver (that might have been difficult, given the relationship between steering wheel, high pedals, and seat). Instruments and minor controls seemed to have been positioned for aesthetic effect, rather than functional efficiency. Some drivers found they could not reach the handbrake with their seat belts secured. Visibility was good.

The early cars were at their best in high-speed cruising, when the efficient engine and body lines combined to improve fuel consumption noticeably. The weight on the front wheels, combined with large Pirelli Cinturato tyres and low gearing, called for muscular effort at low speeds, but the steering became lighter as speed increased. The handling was neutral, cornering powers were high, and there was little body roll. The gearchange was, however, heavy, and reluctant when the 'box was cold. The engine was smooth, so the vibrations most drivers experienced above 150km/h – above 100mph in rounded terms – were put down to an airflow quirk.

Left: This side view of an Espada emphasizes its sleek lines. The interior (above) had four full seats, and the obtrusive central console that featured in front-engined Lamborghinis. It carried air-conditioning ducts. There was little room to spare around the V12 (right).

The claimed top speed of 250km/h (155mph) is another nicely rounded figure, and around 240km/h (150mph) seems more realistic.

Modifications were made through the second half of 1968, as production got under way, and in 1969, notably when a little more rear headroom was found through a floorpan change. There were also odd special versions, including one with a large part of the roof in glass, recalling the Marzal.

The second series Espada was introduced early in 1970, and it ran until 1972. It had a high-compression V12, with quoted power output increased from 325bhp to 350bhp. The transmission and brakes were uprated, and power steering was offered as an overdue option. Inside, there was a more sensible fascia, with all the instruments concentrated ahead of the steering wheel, the speedo and tacho flanking the secondary dials. The wheel was still a relatively large-diameter, thin-rimmed, three-spoke type. There were minor comfort improvements, and the ventilation system was revised.

Late 1972 saw the third series Espada, which was to be continued to 1978. Change was needed, but the state of the company meant that fundamental changes (or a replacement model) could not be undertaken.

The grille was modified, and cars for the US market were to have cumbersome '5mph impact' bumpers at the front, and black rear bumpers. The attractive wheels that had been introduced a little earlier became standard. ZF power steering was specified for all cars, the brakes were uprated again, and there were minor suspension revisions.

At little cost in terms of power, US emissions regulations were met in the mid-1970s. The Chrysler Torqueflite 3-speed automatic transmission was offered from 1974 – not such an oddity for an Italian high-performance car, when Ferruccio Lamborghini's original ambitions for his company's four-seater were recalled.

The fascia was revised again, less satisfactorily this time as symmetry was abandoned to position a radio by the driver's left hand, but the fact that the main instruments were brought more into the line

Below: A broad flat bonnet top, in aluminium incidentally, was an eye-catching detail of the Espada (in this case 9198).

SPECIFICATION	ESPADA SERIES 3
ENGINE	60 degree V12, dohc, 3929cc
HORSEPOWER	350bhp @ 7500rpm
TRANSMISSION	Manual 5-speed, or 3-speed automatic
CHASSIS	Integral
SUSPENSION	Independent front and rear
BRAKES	Disc
TOP SPEED	Claimed 250km/h (155mph)
ACCELERATION	0-100km/h (62mph): 6.9 seconds

of sight was an improvement. Some lesser instruments and switches were sited in a segment angled towards the driver and merging into the top of the transmission tunnel. Other cockpit changes were in details.

The Espada survived the company upheavals through most of the 1970s, and Bertone's body

Above: Mid-'70s cockpit, with angled segment of fascia, left.

lines aged very slowly. The only special-bodied version, Frua's 1978 four-door Faena one-off, served to underline the rare quality of the original.

Aesthetics apart, opinions and critical assessments remained mixed to the end, but qualities such as handling were invariably praised. The Espada complemented the Countach admirably, and production might have continued at a modest level had the Lamborghini company not

Above: The clear panel in the tail was a useful feature.

fallen under court administration in mid-1978. The bodies were made by an outside supplier, and such external commitments were to be avoided when cash-flow was a mere trickle. When production ended, 1217 Espadas had been built in ten years, making it the most successful model in the first quarter of a century of Lamborghini cars.

Lamborghini Islero

THE ISLERO took the place of the 400GT, and was announced at the 1968 Geneva Motor Show, when it was, however, overshadowed by the Espada. Although Ferruccio Lamborghini chose an Islero as his personal car – he had a hand in its subdued styling – it was to be a secondary model through its two-year life. The Islero was a 'businessman's express', with no sporting pretensions, and it was a 2+2 rather than a true four-seater. It thus fell into a market sector then well catered for by manufacturers such as Mercedes-Benz, as well as the more obvious Ferraris with the contemporary Daytona. It was named after a bull that killed a famous matador in 1947 . . .

The Islero was based on the square-tube chassis and suspension of the 350/400, with the same wheelbase (although overall it was shorter) and a fractionally wider track to exploit advances in tyre technology. The V12 seemed to be accommodated more comfortably, and an admirably low bonnet line was achieved, while the steering lock was acceptable. The engine was rated at 320bhp in the first cars, and drove the rear wheels through the Lamborghini 5-speed all-synchro gearbox.

The styling was by Marazzi, a group of Touring personnel displaced when that famous Turin firm went out of business. Outward lines were almost severe, with retractable main lights and thin bumpers enhancing the clean appearance, and single curvature windows instead of the complex glass of earlier cars. It was slightly shorter than the 400GT, but had a little more cabin room. The interior came in for wide criticism for its fittings,

Below: The Islero had notably clean lines, and was obviously an extension of the 350/400 theme.

SPECIFICATION	ISLERO S
ENGINE	60 degree V12, dohc, 3929cc
HORSEPOWER	350bhp @ 7700rpm
TRANSMISSION	Manual 5-speed
CHASSIS	Tubular
SUSPENSION	Independent front and rear
BRAKES	Disc
TOP SPEED	260km/h (162mph)
ACCELERATION	0-100km/h (62mph): 6.3 seconds

which were just too utilitarian for such a car; all the necessary instruments were there, well displayed, but several minor switches were awkwardly positioned (unlike the stubby little gear lever). Poor trim reflected the generally low build quality of the early cars. Some were improved by owners, for example with full-leather seats, and one or two were converted to right-hand drive.

Performance was more highly rated, for the V12 was smooth and responsive, and gave a claimed top speed of 265km/h (165mph), which perhaps translates realistically as 255km/h or 158mph. Handling was responsive and sure, the disc brakes powerful.

About 15 months after the Islero was introduced, and 125 cars on, an S version was announced. Some of the shortcomings were overcome in this, which was distinguished by its gently flared arches for wider tyres, longitudinal vents behind the front wheel arches, and fog lights inset in the grille. The compression ratio of the engine was raised, and with carburettor and inlet manifold modifications the output was increased to 350bhp, to give 260km/h (162mph). The cockpit

was overhauled, with new trim and seats, and a revised fascia.

Its V12 aside, the Islero still lacked the refinement expected of a car in its class, and it was always expensive, the S costing almost as much as the Ferrari Daytona. Just a hundred 'S' were built before production ended early in 1970.

Top and above: This Islero GTS, or S, dates from 1969 and is one of only a hundred built. Most changes were under the skin, and outwardly the variant could be recognized only by details such as the gently flared wheel arches, fog lights inset in the grille and the slot outlet engine air vents. Campagnolo wheels of this pattern were used on several Lamborghini models.

Lamborghini Jarama

THE JARAMA has been described as 'the forgotten Lamborghini' – Ferruccio Lamborghini felt it was the type of car his range needed, but the company's new managers were less keen, so it was only built in modest numbers. It owed its name to an area of Spain notable for fighting bulls (rather than the race circuit).

As the 1960s ended, it was obvious that the Islero would have a short life, and the Jarama was introduced as a successor at the 1970 Geneva Motor Show. It was a 2+2 intended to complement the Espada, with a similar mechanical make-up and a short version of the Espada chassis. It also inherited some of the shortcomings of its stablemate, notably in the cockpit, the driving position and the heavy steering.

It may have been the shortest Lamborghini when it was introduced, but it still had to be wide, for the V12 had to be squeezed in between the front wheels. The two dimensions imposed restrictions on designer Gandini, and the requirement that the car should appear relatively staid to suit its role as a 'businessman's express' imposed more. The outcome was a fastback, which looked sleek from some angles, almost chunky from others.

The aggressive nose was distinguished by partial eyelid covers for the two pairs of quartz halogen headlights. The covers were electrically operated, and in case of hesitant operation the flashing function was handled by the twin driving lights on the bottom line of the grille. The bonnet top was flat, with two NACA inlets for the air conditioning system, similar to those on the Espada.

Inside, the short chassis meant that the rear

Below: The Jarama modified by Bob Wallace, sometimes known as the 400GT Sport.

Below: The Jarama had a very clean profile, and this last front-engined GT Lamborghini compares interestingly with the 350GT. Weight and build quality let it down.

Above: Half-hooded main lights were a bold styling feature.

SPECIFICATION	JARAMA 400 GT
ENGINE	60 degree V12, dohc, 3929cc
HORSEPOWER	350bhp @ 7800rpm
TRANSMISSION	Manual 5-speed
CHASSIS	Integral
SUSPENSION	Independent front and rear
BRAKES	Disc
TOP SPEED	Claimed 260km/h (162mph)
ACCELERATION	0-100km/h (62mph): 6.0 seconds

seats were cramped, but their backs could be lowered to increase the otherwise narrow and shallow luggage space. The front seats were comfortable and supportive, but once again the driver had to suffer the 'Italian driving position'. In the rest of the cockpit, styling seemed to have taken priority over ergonomics, and the finish came in for much criticism.

While Marazzi was responsible for body assembly, Bertone made the panels, in steel – bad news for modern restorers! But despite the high kerb weight of 1630kg (3593lb), which was split 52/48 front/rear, the V12 in 350bhp form propelled the Jarama 400GT to over 240km/h (150mph). No independent testers seemed to have achieved the claimed 260km/h (162mph). Road behaviour was highly rated, in terms of stability and cornering, braking and ride.

The 1972 Geneva Show saw the announcement of the 400GTS, or Jarama S, which had a substantially improved cockpit and engine

uprated to give 365bhp; power steering was to come, and the Torqueflite automatic transmission, as on the Espada. New wheels and a thin, wide, bonnet-top intake between the NACA intakes identified the S. A variant with two removable roof panels, giving a Targa effect, was seen.

In 1972 one car was prepared to near-circuit specification by development engineer Bob Wallace, whose competition car instincts lingered from his days as a racing mechanic. The engine was uprated to produce some 400bhp, and it looked the part with chin aerofoil, big bonnet-top outlets, fat wheels, and outside filler cap, while there were some aluminium body panels and plastics windows, and a stripped interior with roll cage. It was a dead-end experiment, but it survives.

Otherwise the Jarama was neglected until it was dropped in 1976. Production of this last front-engined Lamborghini car – the distinction is needed because of later off-roaders – totalled 177 first-generation 400GTs and 150 400GTS.

Lamborghini Countach

THE SUPERCAR of the 1970s appeared as an improbably futuristic exhibit at the 1971 Geneva Motor Show. But just occasionally motor show fantasy becomes production reality. Bertone's Lancia-powered show car for Turin in 1970 was one such example; it was named Stratos, and it was followed in 1971 by a production version, which went on to dominate world rallying. And the yellow Lamborghini that was the sensation of 1971 was followed by a production car, introduced at Geneva in March 1973, although the first customers did not take delivery until 1974.

The first production version was the LP400 (LP – *Longitudinale Posteriore*, a description of the engine configuration). It was not named for a bull, but, according to one of those nice little asides of motoring history, after a Lamborghini worker's astonished exclamation when he first saw the car, using a term often appreciative of a beautiful woman . . .

It had been initiated simply as Project 112, and following on from the Miura, it owed something to that ground-breaking car. Paolo Stanzani, who had become chief designer and engineer when Dallara left to pursue the racing will-'o-the-wisp, had overall design responsibility and his principal assistant was Massimo Parenti, who had played a major role in refining the Miura. While they stayed with the overall mid-engined configuration of that car, they sought to avoid some of its shortcomings with another original approach.

First and foremost, then, the V12 engine was turned through 90 degrees to a conventional fore-and-aft position. However, the installation was far from conventional, in that the drive was taken forward to a 5-speed gearbox ahead of the engine – almost beside the driver's elbow. It was then stepped down to the propeller shaft and taken back in a straight run through the crankcase, in a sealed tube, to the differential at the rear of the V12. The engine was comfortably within the wheelbase, and the front/rear weight distribution of 42/58 was acceptable, if not ideal. A penalty was a high centre of gravity, as the engine bulk was raised. Development of the unorthodox power train was time-consuming.

Left: Few supercars have invited artistic interpretation like the Countach. . .

SPECIFICATION	COUNTACH LP400
ENGINE	60 degree V12, dohc, 3929cc
HORSEPOWER	375bhp @ 8000rpm
TRANSMISSION	Manual 5-speed
CHASSIS	Multitubular
SUSPENSION	Independent front and rear
BRAKES	Disc
TOP SPEED	Approx 275km/h (171mph)
ACCELERATION	0-100km/h (62mph): 6.9 seconds

The wheelbase might have been expected to be longer than the Miura's. It was shorter; 2450mm (96.5in) compared with 2500mm (98.4in). Overall length was 4140mm (163in) compared with 4370mm (172in), and while the front track was wider, the rear track was a little narrower. Within these dimensions packaging had to be tight, and with machinery taking up much of the space, the Countach was strictly a two-seater.

The first car had a semi-monocoque chassis of square tubes and welded-on panels. It was to be replaced by a complex space-frame of substantial round tubes, used regardless of the high labour costs involved. Production cars had unstressed aluminium bodywork, in place of a steel body. Generally, suspension, steering, brakes and wheels were carried over from the Miura.

Below: Early Countach at rest. Bertone's pure lines have been partly sacrificed to reality.

Below: The large windscreen, prominent intakes, and the roof channel to allow rearward visibility in this 'periscope' Lamborghini show to advantage from above.

37

The Countach S, or LP400S, came in 1978. Outward recognition points included the badging at the rear, wide low-profile tyres, 'phone dial' wheels, extended wheel arches and the little chin spoiler. The basic body did not generate lift, so the rear wing added weight and drag, with no proven aerodynamic benefits. The interior layout (left) was clean, but the cabin was not comfortable for tall people. Conventional doors could well have been impossibly wide, and the system adopted (from a 1968 Bertone concept car) worked well. Dignified entry posed problems.

Left: A right-hand-drive Countach LP500S on the open road. Clear glass covered the turn indicators, with twin pop-up main lights above these panels. Below: Countach concept car. Right: Rear view of an LP500S with a cosmetic rear wing. This car has the 'phone dial' wheels. The lights are neat, and black lettering restrained – some cars had chrome letters and symbols.

The body lines were amazing, and while some modifications were called for as running experience built up, they were not far removed from the original car shown at Geneva in 1971. Gandini took cues from late-1960s sports-racing cars, and the Alfa Romeo-based Bertone Carabo (beetle) of 1968. That was a show car, with a wedge nose and front-hinged doors that opened upwards, which were likened to beetle wings.

Both features were prominent on the Countach. There was a short nose, with a slight change of angle to the large windscreen. The doors turned out to be practical – a Countach was not likely to live in a low-built suburban garage – and opening them proved simple as the weight was taken by pneumatic struts. Complex curvature ruled out wind-down windows, so a small opening panel was provided on each side in the prototype; the door windows of production cars were to be divided horizontally, so that half opened. Escape from an inverted car worried commentators, who were advised that in the unlikely event of a roll, the windscreen should be pushed out!

The lines of that first car were outstandingly pure, uncluttered with intakes or even mirrors, for radiator air was taken in through slats behind the doors, and a central periscope in a roof fairing was to provide rearward vision.

The cockpit echoed the futuristic exterior. There was a single-spoke wheel and warning lights

ahead of it, in the line of sight. These drew attention to any fault, which was specified on a panel to the left. An electronic digital rev counter and speedometer were proposed, but at that time were not reliable. In measured dimensions, the cockpit was a little larger than the Miura's, despite the fuel tanks on each side making for intrusive sills (each tank in the production cars held 60 litres/13.2 gallons). Behind the cockpit, the body lines suggested a large powerplant, while right at the tail the luggage compartment was larger than the

Miura's (and a little soft luggage could also be squeezed in around the spare wheel in the nose). Engine accessibility via a top hatch was not good.

The first car started life with a 5-litre V12 (hence the LP500 designation). Bore and stroke in this unit were increased, but there were worries about its life expectancy, which were justified, as it was to fail during tests, and the 3.9 litre unit was substituted. An exception was made for entrepreneur Walter Wolf, best known for his Grand Prix team, but in the 1970s also a possible Lamborghini backer;

he had an LP400 with a 5-litre engine. The test programme was extensive, and resulted in many changes. Most noticeably, overheating led to additional air intakes, which by production took shape as large shoulder scoops and flush NACA intakes behind the doors. Under the skin, the cooling system had to be reworked. Pre-production cars also had nose modifications to overcome excess downforce, and cockpit fittings became much more conventional. The historic first car was sacrificed in crash tests, in England.

LP400

The V12s of the first production cars were rated at 375bhp, a little less than the Miura P400SV, probably because of a change to six twin-choke side draught carburettors. The chassis was clothed in Lamborghini's first in-house bodywork, which incorporated the revised intakes, and the wide depression in the roof that had been provided when a rear-view 'periscope' was planned (hence early cars are sometimes called 'periscope Countach'). A normal internal rear-view mirror was standard. There were also two driving lights under the nose.

A concealed button inside the NACA ducts released the doors, which swung up easily on single hinges (the awkward fuel filler caps were also in these ducts). Entry was less simple, and once in, there was no spare room, with the sills and gearbox flanking the seats, a low roof, and small footwells (tall drivers found this drawback compounded by the wheel, which forced a splay-leg position). Rev counter and speedo faced the driver, and were flanked by six secondary instruments. Column stalks provided the switch gear for lights, indicators and the single large windscreen wiper. The controls tended to be heavy.

Visibility to the front was good, although the nose was out of sight, but visibility was almost non-existent through the three-quarter rear quadrant.

Top: Federal low-speed impact bumpers made little sense on a car built for high speeds, and ruined the fine nose lines.
Above: The 5-litre V12 engine of the LP500S; the bay is not cluttered but access is tight.

Cockpit noise seemed to vary from car to car, and the engine note took on a 'thoroughbred howl' above about 5000rpm. Air conditioning offset the greenhouse effect of the large 'screen, and ambient warmth from mechanical parts.

Speed also varied from car to car, but no independent tests confirmed the 305km/h (190mph) originally claimed; 275km/h (171mph) was entirely credible. At that, it was an extremely quick car, the fastest production model of the mid-1970s.

Acceleration from standstill to 100mph (about 160km/h) took 13.1 sec, while the standing start kilometre was covered in a fraction over 25 seconds.

Production and sales got under way slowly in 1974, when just 23 cars were delivered. Then the rate picked up, to reach a total of 150 before the LP400S was announced early in 1978.

The principal changes associated with this version were in the chassis and suspension, largely as Pirelli's low-profile P7 tyres were adopted. These gave more grip than the Michelins used earlier, but were squat and wider, and that called for wheel arch extensions. These were in glass fibre, and at the front were in one moulding with a chin spoiler. They merged in neatly, and were finished in the body colour, but in side elevation the angular inside lines of the extensions were in conflict with the wheels – or, depending on taste, gave the Countach a new aggressive appearance. Dallara returned, to rework the suspension.

Above: A quartet of Countach space frames waiting to meet alloy bodies. Right: In the QV, little changed beyond the four-valve (Quattrovalvole) engine, but the improved breathing of that unit helped boost output. The only change at the rear was in the information for following drivers.

Cars destined for the USA had to be fitted with front and rear bumpers, and while these were among the least offensive of the rash brought on by legislation, they did nothing for the looks of the sleek Countach. Side lights were repositioned, just below the main lights. The structure around the cockpit, including the doors, also had to be strengthened for the US market.

A rear aerofoil also became available, and was fitted to the most Series 2 cars; it emphasized high-performance qualities, although the general impression was that it added drag without making a contribution to downforce (it increased the Cd figure to an unimpressive 0.42). The roof was in steel, and the channel intended for the rear-view periscope was discontinued.

The S was slightly lighter, with a kerb weight of 1322kg (2915lb), but there was extra drag and some loss of power, which was down to no more

Below: The last production Countach was the Anniversary QV. The tail legend changed, to just a wreathed '25' and a bull on the flat panel and a discreet 'Lamborghini' on the back of the engine deck . . .

Left: . . . and how much prettier it looks with minimal embellishment, intakes in the body colour and those Ferrari-like strakes where air is fed to the wheels.

would not have met emissions regulations a dozen years on. This was a 4754cc unit. Bore and stroke were increased, from 82 x 62mm to 85.5 x 69mm, and the compression ratio was reduced to 9.1:1. This restored the output to 375bhp at 7000rpm – 1000rpm less than the 4-litre engine – while torque was appreciably improved. The performance gain was in recovery, top speed being some 280km/h (174mph), without that cosmetic rear aerofoil. To justify claims that the Countach was the world's fastest production car, more power was needed.

Giulio Alfieri had joined Lamborghini to rework the V8, and had then been responsible for engineering the LP500S, before developing a 'super Countach' that would reach the magic 300km/h (186mph). The chassis and body were retained – fragile company resources in the early 1980s could not justify anything new in those areas – and work was concentrated on the V12, with some transmission refinement to come.

than 350bhp in 'European' cars, while the output of engines in US-specification cars was as little as 325bhp. A turbo version was mooted, but not seriously pursued (an independent tuner did produce a turbo conversion).

There were a few detail cockpit changes, and new instruments introduced during the production life of the S were neatly arranged in a rectangular panel. Door mirrors may have signified another erosion of the pure lines, but they were a boon . . .

The LP400S was in production through another period of company upheavals, and the 385 built made a major contribution to the survival of Lamborghini, as the Mimran brothers gained outright control.

LP500S

The larger V12 that was introduced in the LP500S in the Spring of 1982 was not the 5-litre engine that had been seen in the first Countach LP500. That

SPECIFICATION	COUNTACH LP500S
ENGINE	60 degree V12, dohc, 4754cc
HORSEPOWER	375bhp @ 7000rpm
TRANSMISSION	Manual 5-speed
CHASSIS	Multitubular
SUSPENSION	Independent front and rear
BRAKES	Disc
TOP SPEED	Approx 280km/h (174mph)
ACCELERATION	0-100km/h (62mph): 5.7 seconds

SPECIFICATION	QUATTROVALVOLE
ENGINE	60 degree V12, dohc, 5167cc
HORSEPOWER	455bhp @ 7000rpm
TRANSMISSION	Manual 5-speed
CHASSIS	Multitubular
SUSPENSION	Independent front and rear
BRAKES	Disc
TOP SPEED	Approx 290km/h (180mph)
ACCELERATION	0-100km/h (62mph): 5.2 seconds

The capacity of the engine was increased to 5167cc (85.5 x 75mm). There was a new four-valve cylinder head with pent-roof combustion chambers, and six vertical twin-choke downdraught Weber carburettors. This Countach Quattrovalvole engine (LP112D) produced 455bhp at 7000rpm, a 21 per cent increase. Cars for the US market had Bosch fuel injection, and a 35bhp drop in power was reflected in a lower top speed – a fact that was near-academic in view of the widespread 55mph speed limit in that country.

During its production life, the Countach QV also gained a gearbox with ZF-type synchromesh.

As with the LP500S, there were minor cockpit improvements, while the new carburettors meant that the engine deck had to be revised. Otherwise the QV was distinguished by discreet tail lettering.

In performance, the QV almost lived up to aims and claims, with 295km/h (183mph) reportedly achieved on a test track, and 288km/h (179mph) recorded in an authoritative road test. Briefly, the Countach took the fastest road car title back from Ferrari.

There were special cars, as far as the factory was concerned notably Walter Wolf's in the 1970s, with distinctive aerofoils and cosmetic touches, and a laboratory car near the end of the model's life. This Evoluzione Countach had unmistakable Countach lines, but the main central structure was in carbon fibre/Kevlar, combined with aluminium doors and wings. Composites saved weight, and the interior was not furnished for a customer, so this car was some 300kg (661lb) lighter than a normal QV. Its engine was carefully prepared, to give 20bhp more than the normal QV unit. The claimed top

speed was 320km/h (199mph) in 1988, when Lamborghini claimed 299km/h (186mph) for the normal QV.

The last cars were labelled 'Anniversary'; build quality was obviously much better than the early cars, as it should have been for a machine for rich customers.

The Countach may have lived beyond its time in some respects – partly because it was so difficult to replace. It underpinned Lamborghini's survival, and when the last of the Anniversary models left Sant'Agata in 1990, its shape was still extraordinary. Few cars can have brought their manufacturer so much admiration.

47

Opposite top: The last Countach (12085) on line 1 in the assembly shop in 1990.

Opposite below: A carburettor V12, ready to be mated to the transmission (the gearbox will be to the right).

Above: The assembly shop was normally squeaky clean, here as gleaming Anniversary models near completion.

Lamborghini Urraco

A 'SMALL' car had been considered essential to the Lamborghini range from the earliest days of the company, but the first did not enter production until 1972. This 'young bull' (Urraco) was not particularly small, with dimensions close to its Ferrari, Maserati and Porsche rivals in an important market class. Lamborghini never achieved the volume production hoped for with this model.

Once the Miura was established, the Espada had been launched, and the Jarama was set to enter production, Paolo Stanzani was able to commit design and development effort to this 'small' bread-and-butter model, in 1969. The basic layout followed that of the Miura, with a transverse mid-mounted engine, but in most other respects the car was new. First and foremost, the engine was a light 90 degree V8 with single overhead camshafts driven by toothed belts, then still novel and somewhat troublesome at first. The engine was deliberately simpler than Lamborghini's V12, cheaper to build and maintain, yet just as efficient – in bhp/litre terms, it matched the larger engine. It was also compact, so that the gearbox could be positioned conventionally, in line with the crankshaft (and on the left in the car so unequal length driveshafts had to be used). The gear linkage was less complicated than the Miura's. The engine/transmission assembly was mounted on a detachable tubular sub-frame.

There was a steel unitary chassis, and the suspension used MacPherson struts all round, with the consequent possible problems involved in having them at the rear accepted as a trade-off for interior space gains. These problems were ironed out during development, and handling was predictable as well as appropriate to a high-performance car. The gains were substantial, for although the Urraco was 90mm (3.5in) shorter than the Miura it had a 2+2 cockpit.

Bertone was again responsible for the lines, the production version differing quite markedly from the first prototype. The appearance was notably clean, with a short nose and long cabin which tailed off with a fastback line. There was a slender chrome bumper above the secondary lights (later US-market cars had larger 'black bumpers'), and retractable headlights atop the nose. Two deep slats in the cover of the nose compartment provided an exit for radiator air, and later gave way to six smaller slats, neater but robbing the nose of some 'character'. This compartment housed the spare wheel, battery and reservoirs for brake, clutch and 'screen washer, with no room for luggage. However, the boot in the tail was reasonably large.

The engine installation ahead of it looked neat, but tight packaging meant that the V8 was not very accessible. The engine cover had to be lifted to gain access to the fuel filler cap – an odd little price to pay for clean lines!

Lamborghini's 'small' engine was the V8 for the Urraco.

Top and above: The Urraco appeared as a rival to Ferrari's Dino 308, and there were even visual resemblances. Here in its definitive P250 form, the Urraco was a well-proportioned GT car.

The interior of the P250 cars was neat, but there were shortcomings – the familiar ones such as a driving position most suitable for an oddly-proportioned person with very short legs and very long arms, a steeply raked windscreen that made for good forward visibility but rapid cockpit temperature rise on sunny days (the optional air conditioning was really necessary), and poor rearward visibility. Most drivers felt that the low and narrow seats were not sufficiently supportive. The two at the rear were small and very upright, so that while a third person could travel in reasonable comfort sitting across them, they were hardly adequate for two adults on a journey of any length.

Unusually, the two main instruments were located at each end of the array facing the driver, with six secondary instruments and sundry warning lights in a row between them. Controls were generally well positioned, but some were rated heavy, especially the lower gears in the 5-speed 'box.

Throughout, build quality showed that Lamborghini was coming to grips with this important aspect of manufacture, with benefits stemming from more work undertaken in-house. The cockpit gave an impression of quality when the car was new, although some of the material used proved to have poor wear rates. The P250S had the desirable tinted glass and electric window lifts, as well as leather seats.

The Urraco was announced late in 1970, but the first production car did not reach a customer until mid-1972, and in that year only 35 were completed. The effective delay of three years was costly . . .

However, in its first P250 form, the Urraco

was well received, as a genuine GT car. Its 2463cc V8 was rated at 220bhp at 7500 rpm, some 35bhp less than the 3-litre V8 in Ferrari's Dino 308 GT4, the obvious 2+2 rival, that appeared in 1973. The Lamborghini was a 230km/h (143mph) car, quicker than a Porsche 911S, Alfa Romeo Montreal or Maserati Merak, but as much as 20km/h (12mph) slower than a Dino 308 GT4.

Handling and roadholding were of a high order, the ride was good and there was little roll in hard cornering. Noise levels were acceptable, but while a hard-revving engine may have been music to some ears, it could be anti-social to outsiders.

Below: Engine access was restricted. This car is the more powerful P300 that was introduced in 1974.

SPECIFICATION	URRACO P250
ENGINE	90 degree V8, sohc, 2463cc
HORSEPOWER	220bhp @ 7500rpm
TRANSMISSION	Manual 5-speed
CHASSIS	Unitary, on platform
SUSPENSION	Independent front and rear
BRAKES	Disc
TOP SPEED	Approx 230km/h (143mph)
ACCELERATION	0-100km/h (62mph): 7.2 seconds

Above: Urraco P250S had higher equipment levels, and the 'black bumpers' on cars for the USA were neatly integrated.

Below: There was less leather in the cockpit of the 'small Lamborghini', and the main instruments were oddly placed.

Sales remained low in 1973, when market conditions had turned against high-performance cars. The possibility that Urraco sales would reach the thousand-a-year mark that had once been projected was remote; the new owners of the company could at least financially write down the considerable costs of preparing for production at that rate, but for the future the car had to be priced higher to reflect economic reality. Consequently, it also had to be uprated to meet the competition from other manufacturers. Hence the P300 introduced at the 1974 Turin Motor Show.

P300

As in other model designations, P indicated the engine position (*posteriore*), and the numerals the engine capacity. The engine in the P300 was much more than an enlarged V8, for it had new cylinder heads and chain-driven twin overhead camshafts. Bore was unchanged at 86mm but the stroke was increased from 53mm to 64.5mm, to give a capacity of 2996cc. The claimed output was 250bhp at 7500rpm, which was increased to 265bhp at 7800rpm in 1976.

The P300 was improved in details of transmission and suspension, and the cabin was to be revised (the speedometer and rev counter were still sited to left and right, but they were moved closer to the wheel as two minor instruments were dropped, and they were angled towards the driver). The P300 was actually cheaper than the P250S which continued production through 1976. The 2.5

litre sohc engine was also retained for the US market, with anti-emissions equipment reducing the power output to 180bhp.

In its P300 form the Urraco had performance to match its road manners. The factory claimed a top speed to 265km/h (165mph), but a good independent road-test figure was 254km/h (158mph).

At the 1974 Turin show, incidentally, Lamborghini had also introduced the P200 for the Italian market. This tax-break special had a 1994cc (77.4 x 53mm) sohc V8, rated at 182bhp. The claimed top speed was 215km/h (134mph). As well as allowing substantial tax savings, the P200 was almost 10 per cent cheaper than the P250; sales reached 66.

Below: There were only tiny exterior changes in the P300. Driving lights under the slender bumper were normal.

Racing enthusiasts were excited as Bob Wallace developed an Urraco prototype for competition after Stanzani had left the company. He worked along predictable lines, stripping the interior, modifying the suspension and fitting wider wheels, adding a front air dam and rear spoiler, modifying the engine to give 310bhp, and devising a 6-speed transmission. It was described as a rally car, although it would hardly have been suitable for that activity. It was raced once, by Wallace in a minor

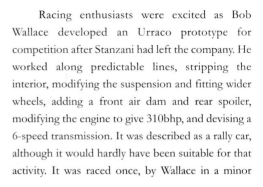

Italian event. That outing was successful, but led nowhere, and soon Wallace left Lamborghini.

The Bravo concept car of 1974 was an 'official' project, using a shortened Urraco chassis. It was designed by Gandini, and was notable for its large glass areas, its curiously asymmetric rear wheel arches (and round front arches!), and fussy detailing. It was extensively tested, and seemed destined for production. Fuel and company crises put paid to that.

In the final P300 version, the Urraco was a good GT car. But its development had been sluggish and sales never reached the level expected, being especially disappointing in the USA. Production of the P250 reached 520 units, and while the P300 was listed for four years only 205 were built. It deserved better . . .

Right: A P300 at Goodwood. Below: Bertone's Bravo on an Urraco basis introduced this wheel style.

53

Lamborghini Silhouette

THIS attractive two-seater was a derivative of the Urraco, with exciting potential that was never realized. It appeared early in 1976, at the Geneva show, when its aggressive lines caused a stir . . . then some shortcomings became known.

It was conceived because a budget to develop the 'baby Countach' Bravo concept car to production form was out of the question. Economy meant that the basic Urraco body shell had to be retained in the Silhouette, and that compromised the lines and the two-seater concept (use of the existing floorpan and windscreen largely defined the cockpit, where the only real revision possible was the deletion of the rear seats).

Bertone worked its magic, and the car 'looked more different than it was'. Compared with an Urraco, there was a large nose air dam incorporating oil cooler and driving lights, there were squared-off and flared wheel arches and the 'telephone dial' wheels from the Bravo, and there was a long, gently tapered tail with its focal points in shoulder scoops for engine air. The basic structure was stiffened, for apart from earlier one-off conversions such as the roadster 350GT and Miura, the Silhouette was the first open Lamborghini. It featured a Targa top, which was neat but apparently all too prone to leak.

Generally, the cockpit gave an impression of being more refined that the Urraco's, but it was let down visually by the fitment of the odd four-spoke steering wheel from the P300. The two main instruments were conventionally located ahead of the driver, flanked by secondary dials. There was space for luggage behind the seats.

The engine was the dohc V8, in 3-litre form, driving through the normal 5-speed gearbox (with a slightly higher top gear ratio). The factory claimed a top speed of more than 250km/h (155mph).

The Silhouette was never the hoped-for competitor for the Ferrari 308GTB which started life with a considerable edge in the respect of Pininfarina's superb body lines. Beyond that, the Lamborghini was under-developed, build quality was not always good, and reliability was suspect. The factory made no effort to modify it to comply with US regulations, and so a market where it might have sold well was ignored, apparently to save the costs of certification. The Silhouette was allowed to fade away in 1978, after only 52 had been made.

Below: Bertone improved on the Urraco in the noselines of the Silhouette.

SPECIFICATION	SILHOUETTE
ENGINE	90 degree V8, dohc, 2996cc
HORSEPOWER	265bhp @ 7800rpm
TRANSMISSION	Manual 5-speed
CHASSIS	Unitary
SUSPENSION	Independent front and rear
BRAKES	Disc
TOP SPEED	Approx 250km/h (155mph)
ACCELERATION	0-100km/h (62mph): 5.6 seconds

Bertone's Athon ('Hymn to the Sun') show car of 1980 was built on a Silhouette chassis. This roadster had futuristic detailing – and no provision at all for a soft top! It underwent some testing, perhaps more for publicity than for development purposes, as there were no funds available to progress it towards production, even if that had been an intention . . .

Below: A Silhouette with the roof panel in place. The black shoulder intakes were a clever styling detail.

Above: Bertone's Athon two-seater roadster was a functioning concept car.

Lamborghini Jalpa

ECHANICALLY, Jalpa derived from Urraco and visually it closely followed Silhouette, and it was to become the most successful model in Lamborghini's V8 line. In fact, this line was allowed to lapse for three years after the Silhouette was dropped, for although Jalpa was shown in 'prototype' form at Geneva in 1981 it was not in production until 1982. It sold well for the rest of the decade, with annual production peaking at some 200 units before it dwindled to a handful in 1991. Jalpa, incedentally, is another fighting bull.

While Lamborghini was in administrative receivership, little or no R & D work was possible, but when the Mimran brothers took control of the company the Jalpa programme got the go-ahead.

Most of the available finance was devoted to mechanical uprating; there were minor body changes, but the overall lines were still open to criticism – the car still rode on a wheelbase dating from the 2+2 Urraco laid down at the end of the 1960s.

Giulio Alfieri, a gifted automotive engineer in a rich Italian tradition, had been persuaded to leave Maserati, and his first Lamborghini task was to revise the V8. The basic make-up – light alloy construction, twin overhead camshafts and two valves per cylinder – was unchanged, and carburettors were still used (four twin-choke downdraught Webers). But the stroke was increased to enlarge the unit, to 3485cc (86 x 75mm). It was a

free-revving engine, up to its 7500rpm red line, with a maximum power rating of 255bhp at 7000rpm. That remained unchanged through the 1980s.

The suspension using MacPherson struts with lower wishbones and coil springs/dampers all round was revised in detail. This suited the low-profile Pirelli P7s which were mounted on 7.5in rim Campagnolo wheels that were much more attractive than the Silhouette's, with those pronounced holes. There was still no assistance for the rack-and-pinion steering, but with a 43/57 front to rear weight distribution it was hardly needed, and certainly not at high speeds.

All pictures: Rich red admirably suits this 1985 Jalpa. This model was the most refined of the small V8-powered types, mechanically and visually, and was deservedly the most successful. Everything comes together neatly, even the 'black bumpers' at the front.

56

SPECIFICATION	JALPA
ENGINE	90 degree V8, dohc, 3485cc
HORSEPOWER	255bhp @ 7000rpm
TRANSMISSION	Manual 5-speed
CHASSIS	Unitary
SUSPENSION	Independent front and rear
BRAKES	Disc
TOP SPEED	Approx 233km/h (145mph)
ACCELERATION	0-100km/h (62mph): 6.5 seconds

The wheels were the most obvious outward change. The air dam at the nose was tidier, and the rear quarters looked surprisingly different on those cars with body-colour intakes, rather than the contrasting black which appeared on the Silhouette and some Jalpas.

This was another two-seater, of course. The space at the back of the cockpit was intended to house the Targa roof panel, but was still useful for luggage. The cockpit was more attractive than the Silhouette's, although the seats were none too generous, narrow and low and for a short driver thus oddly positioned in relation to the high steering wheel (which, after the cheap wheel fitted to Silhouette, was a nice three-spoke wheel). Ergonomic awareness showed in the layout of fascia and minor controls. Speedometer and rev counter were ahead of the driver, with an oil pressure gauge between them, while the fuel gauge and two temperature gauges were on the centre line. The gearchange was still heavy, as was the clutch.

Lamborghini claimed a 248km/h (154mph) top speed, but reliable independent road tests failed to confirm this, the best achieving 233km/h (145mph). Among obvious rivals, the slightly more expensive 3.2 litre Ferrari 328GTS was a 260km/h (162mph) car, while the more expensive 3.2 litre Porsche 911 Targa had a 238km/h (148mph) top speed. The Jalpa covered a standing start kilometre in 26.8 sec, and the claimed 0-100km/h figure was 6.5 sec, which approximates to an independent test's 6.2 sec 0-60mph time.

The ride was firm, handling was good, and the ventilated disc brakes were very efficient. It was not a quiet car at high cruising speeds, with excessive wind noise in 'open' or 'closed' forms. Visibility to the front was good, but, in common with its forerunners, very poor in some rear quarters (although the shallow rear window gave good visibility directly back).

The Jalpa looked like an Italian high-

performance car, and it sounded like one – two qualities that could not be measured, but which were important to buyers assessing it alongside sports/GT cars from more northerly European countries. It also extended the useful life of the production facilities laid down for the Urraco (presumably already written down financially, in any case) and it admirably complemented the Countach in the 1980s.

A Jalpa was the basis for the Portofino concept car of 1987, which rates a footnote in the Lamborghini story as a four-door car. It was the first tangible product of the Chrysler take-over, and to a degree it followed an earlier Chrysler design (the pillarless Chrysler 300 of 1993 completed the circle). The Portofino's four doors opened skywards like the Countach's, the front pair hinged at the front, the rear pair at the rear. There were no B

Opposite top: Lamborghini's claims that the ergonomic shortcomings of the Silhouette cockpit had been overcome in the Jalpa were not entirely borne out. . . Opposite below: The Jalpa not only looked like an Italian high-performance car, it could also manage a very respectable top speed of around 233km/h (145mph). Below The extraordinary Portofino concept car of 1987 demonstrating its skywards-opening doors.

pillars, so the chassis was probably not too rigid. Nothing came of the Portofino, which is retained by MascoTech Special Vehicles in the USA.

Enthusiasts anticipated an open sports car version of the Jalpa, speculating on a model following the lines of Bertone's Athon study. Nothing came of that, and hints about the next possible replacement might be found in the Cala.

This appeared in the P140/L140 evolution, both projects conceived around a V10 engine, which implied that the Jalpa marked the end of Lamborghini's V8 family. It had served the company well – it did not fall between stools like the Urraco, nor had it gained a dubious reputation in areas like build quality that had dogged the Silhouette, and it had found acceptance in the USA.

Lamborghini Cala

IN THE late 1980s, Chrysler looked to a new, small Lamborghini as a possible successor to the Jalpa to run with the Diablo in the 1990s. Prototype chassis designated P140 were built to a design by Luigi Marmiroli, but the project was shelved in 1992.

Under MegaTech ownership, the possibility was revived as L140 and Lamborghini invited studios to submit body designs. The Cala was carried through to a working show car. It was first seen on the ItalDesign stand at the 1995 Geneva Motor Show, but at events later that year (for

example, the London Motor Show) it appeared on a Lamborghini stand. Lamborghini attributed the design to Fabrizio Giugiaro, while outsiders detected contributions by his illustrious father.

There were echoes of past cars in this 2+2 – the Countach-style windscreen, Miura-inspired headlights, Jalpa-like removable roof panel. An aluminium platform chassis carried the carbon-fibre and aluminium body, which in its general lines and detailing tended to be softer and more rounded than past Lamborghinis. Overall, it was short and high

alongside the Diablo, and the 2+2 description was optimistic . . .

The 3.9 litre V10 engine was rated at 400bhp, and it drove through a 6-speed gearbox.

The aim was 'an exclusive high-performance small sports car suitable for everyday driving'. There was no denying the stunning good looks of the Cala, but we may have to wait until the turn of the century to see if it will become a production reality.

All pictures: P140 got off to a false start, was set aside in 1992, and re-emerged with the Cala name in 1995, still as a concept car. ItalDesign came up with a stunning confection, short and compact, with a riot of curves, and dark windows and intakes to set off bright yellow bodywork.

Lamborghini Diablo

THE SUCCESSOR to the Countach was every inch as spectacular as the legendary 1971 supercar – in may respects Lamborghini more than matched it in the Diablo. This was its first car to reach the magic 200mph (322km/h), and it was proclaimed as a true production model – unlike the limited edition Ferrari F40. Lamborghini's fortunes were to rest on it through the last decade of the 20th century, although it was never to be built in the numbers optimistically envisaged – at least 500 a year was the target when it was launched. Its derivatives were to be more advanced than any Countach, and it was to be the first sports Lamborghini to be raced 'officially' as the company belatedly recognized the image benefits to be gained from motor sport . . .

The Diablo was unveiled at Monte Carlo in January 1990, before the last few cars in the Countach Anniversary run were completed, and when only prototype and pre-production Diablos had been built. Real production was still months away, at the end of a long gestation period.

The technical director responsible for the new car was Luigi Marmiroli, who had been attracted away from Alfa Romeo to design it. Work on the

Below: The Diablo succeeded the Countach, and lived up to it in every inch of its svelte lines.

project with the type number 132 began early in 1986, and just over a year later the first prototype was completed (at that time, incidentally, the name Diablo was chosen, specifically for a famous Spanish fighting bull, but by happy chance travelling internationally as 'devil'). There was an interlude as Chrysler took over Lamborghini, and then required design modifications, so that the first definitive prototype did not run until mid-1989.

Several Italian studios were invited to design the body, but almost inevitably Marcello Gandini was commissioned (his Bertone days behind him, he was by then a freelance, and the finished car was to carry his badge).

Broadly, the construction evolved from the Countach, but the welded tubes of the space-frame were square; this simplified production, and the chassis was reckoned to be 30 per cent stiffer than the Countach round-tube frame in torsion. Front and rear were designed as 'crumple zones', while high-strength steel was used for the cockpit safety cell, and tougher alloys were used for the doors. There was some use of carbon-fibre composites, drawing on experience with the Evoluzione Countach, notably in the central tunnel as well as some body panels.

The double wishbone and coil spring independent suspension was redesigned for this car, while the intention to introduce four-wheel drive, and the possibility that ABS and an active suspension system might be adopted were also taken into consideration.

The classic V12 was reworked to such an extent that a new type number (521) was justified. Bore and stroke were increased (to 87 x 80mm) to

Above: The fuel injection engine looks very tidy compared with earlier V12s. Right: The Diablo was particularly sleek in side elevation.

give a capacity of 5707cc, and electronic fuel injection was adopted. The original target output was 460bhp, but when the Diablo was introduced the engine was rated at 492bhp at 7000rpm, with torque increased from 276lb/ft in the late Countach to 428lb/ft, both at 5200rpm. Importantly, twin catalytic converters were standard, and the engine met emissions requirements in all markets.

There was a new 5-speed gearbox, designed from the outset to be used with the transfer box of the four-wheel-drive Diablo that was yet to come. Also in the future was a traction control system, introduced on the 1993 Special Edition cars that marked Lamborghini's 30 years in car manufacture.

The Diablo was a large car by the 1990s supercar standards set by Ferrari and McLaren, albeit their cars tended to be more specialized – it

was 4460mm (175.5in) long and 2040mm (80.3in) wide. So it was a credit to Gandini that it did not look bulky (as, say, the Jaguar XJ220 most certainly did). Compared with the Countach, the wheelbase was longer and the track wider, making for handling improvements as well as greater internal space. It was also considerably heavier, at 1651kg (3640lb), compared with the 1487kg (3278lb) Countach.

Overall, there were strong visual resemblances,

for although the Diablo had much smoother lines, the short nose/long tail appearance of the Countach was retained, together with features such as the front-hinged swing-up doors. American bumper requirements were taken into account at the

Below: An early Diablo at the factory, with a Countach awaiting attention behind it, and LMs to draw attention to the supercar's slippery lines.

design stage, so the add-on impression of black bumpers was avoided; the rear bumper, mounted clear of the bodywork, doubled as an aerodynamic aid, but the rear spoiler offered as an extra served no useful purpose, adding drag and impairing rearward visibility that was already marginal. Intakes for engine and brake air were neatly integrated, and the big rear-mounted radiators meant that nose apertures were not needed (the aluminium water radiators flanked the fuel tank). The 0.31 drag coefficient was considerably better than the 0.40 of the Countach.

In this Lamborghini the boot was in the nose; it was accessible and almost roomy by earlier standards. There was no provision for a spare wheel – not even a space-saver . . .

The cockpit was roomier than the Countach cabin, too, but the familiar footwell restrictions remained. This Lamborghini had an adjustable steering column, which combined with seat adjustment so that a comfortable laid-back driving position was possible. The two main instruments were again at the sides of the panel, which meant they could be partly hidden by hands on the wheel. There was much high-quality leather – too much for some purists, who felt that function should take priority over luxury in a car like this – while air conditioning and electric windows were standard fittings. An effort was made to provide storage space in the cockpit, but shallow pockets in doors that open upwards were not a very good idea . . .

The interior design was credited to Chrysler, whose studio had to work within the limits imposed by the windscreen, the doors, and the intrusive central tunnel housing the gearbox.

Complete V12 engines (above), automotive in the foreground and marine units behind, and (right) blocks which show their different sizes.

The claimed top speed in 1990 was 325km/h (202mph). Like the acceleration figures, this was fractionally better than Ferrari's best figures for the F40, but the maximum speed was confirmed in an independent American test. Generally, road behaviour was highly rated, although handling did attract criticism, and – as ever! – the steering was very heavy at low speeds. And alongside the Ferrari, its size told against it.

Diablo VT

The announcement of the four-wheel-drive Diablo VT (Viscous Traction) came in 1991, although this version did not go on sale until 1993. The existing transmission layout with the gearbox ahead of the engine was well suited to four-wheel drive, and the power was carried to the front wheels via a centre differential. A maximum of 29 percent of the power was fed through the front wheels, and in normal driving conditions the VT was virtually a rear-wheel-drive car, with power directed automatically to the front wheels if traction was lost at the rear.

The VT also had 'staged dampers', with four manual settings or an automatic mode, when the system was governed by vehicle speed. The automatic system could over-ride a driver-selected 'soft' setting if speed exceeded a programmed limit, adopting a stiffer or more 'sporty' ride. Power-assisted steering that was weighted to match speeds was welcomed, proving precise under most driving conditions.

Generally, testers found that handling qualities were improved, although the need for anti-lock braking was emphasized. The VT was heavier than the first Diablo, so no faster.

By 1995 the cockpit had been improved, in details of the fascia and minor controls, and in the air conditioning.

The next variant to appear was the roadster, shown at Geneva in 1992 with a very open cockpit

Below: A four-wheel-drive VT on the Goodwood start line in 1994, ready for the short sprint up the hill. From this angle there was nothing to distinguish it from a rear-wheel-drive Diablo.

SPECIFICATION	DIABLO VT
ENGINE	60 degree V12, dohc, 5707cc
HORSEPOWER	492bhp @ 6850rpm
TRANSMISSION	Manual 5-speed
CHASSIS	Multi-tubular
SUSPENSION	Independent front and rear
BRAKES	Disc
TOP SPEED	Claimed 325km/h (202mph)
ACCELERATION	0-100km/h (62mph): 4.0 seconds

and shallow windscreen. Production was promised for 1993 – ironically, the year when German conversions company Koenig offered an open Diablo, converted from an existing closed car.

The production roadster based on the VT was in fact a Targa-top car, recalling the Jalpa. Its carbon-fibre roof panel could be stowed over the engine cover, located by two pivots and secured by an 'electropneumatic' system that could be activated only when the car was stationary. There was an effective full windscreen. The bracing needed to maintain rigidity – in the A pillars, the sills, across the rear of the cockpit and so on – and an integral

SPECIFICATION	DIABLO SE30
ENGINE	60 degree V12, dohc, 5707cc
HORSEPOWER	525bhp @ 7100rpm
TRANSMISSION	Manual 5-speed
CHASSIS	Multi-tubular
SUSPENSION	Independent front and rear
BRAKES	Disc
TOP SPEED	Claimed 331km/h (206mph)
ACCELERATION	0-100km/h (62mph): 3.9 seconds

roll-over bar pushed the weight up again, and no performance improvements were claimed. Incidentally, Lamborghini suggested that the open car was actually stiffer than the closed version.

The SE30 in 1993 was a purposeful 'special edition', with production limited to 30 units, to mark the 30th anniversary of the first Lamborghini car. It had drive to the rear wheels only, and had a 525bhp engine to propel a car that was some 10 per cent lighter than the normal Diablo. There was

Above: SE30 was a limited-run 'special edition', with modest competitions potential.

traction control, developed by Lamborghini engineering and based on its Formula 1 technology. More parts were in carbon fibre, and in the engine there was some magnesium in the cylinder heads. Some features such as adjustable anti-roll bars, four-point seat harness and roll-over bar suggested competitions use.

Outwardly, the nose was changed a little, to gain an aerodynamic advantage, and a rear aerofoil with an adjustable flap was standard. An engine cover with transverse louvres recalling models back to the Miura followed the lines of the overall bodywork. The door windows had small inset opening sections, to save the weight of full opening gear, and the cockpit was more spartan. Lamborghini claimed a 331km/h (206mph) maximum speed, with 0-100km/h (62mph) acceleration in 4.0 seconds. Each SE30 carried a numbered plate, below the left window.

This model showed a growing awareness of the value of racing experience to a supercar manufacturer, and with an eye to private entrants in national GT championships, a further developed engine and other competitions-related parts were offered. This trend gained impetus with the Diablo SV, which succeeded the SE in 1996.

That year, incidentally, a hydraulic lifting system was introduced at the front, which enabled the driver to raise the nose by 45mm (1.8in), to match rear ground clearance. The car was automatically returned to normal configuration when road speed reached 70km/h (44mph).

In some respects the SV (Sport Veloce) could be regarded as a simplified car, for there were fewer carbon-fibre components, the electronic damper adjustment had been set aside, the V12 did not have magnesium parts and was less highly tuned, giving

Left: A VT roadster.

510bhp. But it had lower gearing, so the drop in top speed to 300km/h (186mph) – almost a theoretical figure, in any case, attainable only on a track – was less significant than the improved acceleration. There were OZ alloy wheels and big Brembo brakes – but no anti-lock system – there were twin engine air intakes proud above the roof line, and there was that unattractive rear aerofoil to go with a rather garish colour scheme. The cockpit was largely black, with plastics trim rather than leather, and a niggardly equipment level. A dignified entry was impossible . . .

The SV was a demanding car to drive – almost a throwback to an earlier supercar era, and far removed from the types of GT car or businessman's express that Ferruccio Lamborghini envisaged for his company. It was also substantially cheaper than other specialist Diablos.

The transformation was taken a stage further in the SV-R, purpose-built for the Philippe Charriol Super Sport Trophy race series. The SV-R had

Above and right: Two views show how neatly the roof stowed.

strengthened chassis, racing suspension, wider wheels and racing disc brakes, and a roll cage, while power-assisted steering and brakes were retained. There was some weight reduction, to 1385kg (3053lb) unladen, while quoted power was up to 540bhp again. Teams entering the series also received a 'racing kit' including aerodynamic parts, safety equipment, and an exhaust system that largely accounted for the power uprating, quick-lift jacks, racing seat and six-point driver harness. They were to be allowed freedom in suspension geometry settings, but engine, gearbox, differential and electronics were sealed.

Although this SV-R and its series was hardly a challenge to other marques, it was well removed from Ferruccio Lamborghini's firm 'no racing' policy. It was also important to the survival of the Diablo until its successor was ready, through the period when it could be the last of the big supercars . . .

SPECIFICATION	DIABLO SV-R
ENGINE	60 degree V12, dohc, 5707cc
HORSEPOWER	540bhp @ 7100rpm
TRANSMISSION	Manual 5-speed
CHASSIS	Multi-tubular
SUSPENSION	Independent front and rear
BRAKES	Disc
TOP SPEED	Approx 305km/h (190mph)
ACCELERATION	N/A

The Diablo SV appeared as a sports Lamborghini, with some raw qualities that took it out of the Road GT category. SV decals are here, there and everywhere from the flanks to the seat backs (below). The combination of suede and plastics in the cockpit (right) was a little odd, too, but there are good clear instruments. The aerodynamic aids earn their place at the back of this Lamborghini (below right). Opposite: The nearest door hides one of the top air intakes for the V12. Racing-style alloy wheels mount really wide (18in) Pirellis at the rear.

SPECIFICATION	DIABLO SV
ENGINE	V12, dohc, 5707cc
HORSEPOWER	510bhp @ 7100rpm
TRANSMISSION	Manual 5-speed
CHASSIS	Space frame
SUSPENSION	Independent front and rear
BRAKES	Disc
TOP SPEED	300km/h (186mph)
ACCELERATION	0-100km/h (62mph): 4.2 seconds

Lamborghini LM 002

THE MASSIVE LM vehicles were at the other end of the motoring spectrum from Lamborghini's sleek cars, but no less exclusive, and in the off-road world most certainly not sluggish. The series started life as a military vehicle project in 1977, when any work was welcome at Sant'Agata and Lamborghini was contracted to build an 'oversize Jeep' by Mobility Technology International.

The programme was cut short when one vehicle had been built. Named Cheetah, it was basic (and large), and powered by a rear-mounted 5.9 litre Chrysler V8, which drove through an automatic transmission. It was apparently written off during tests, and whiffs of scandals lingered – another US company successfully applied for injunctions against MTI on the grounds of patent infringement, while stories in Italy suggested that funds allocated to Lamborghini's collaboration with BMW had been misapplied to the Cheetah . . .

However, the ground work was available when the Mimrans took over, and Lamborghini showed a new prototype in 1981, designated LM 001 (assumed to stand for *Lamborghini Militari*). It was proposed that this would be available with a Lamborghini V12 or an AMC V8, mounted at the rear. The weight distribution made for uncertain steering.

The third attempt was front-engined, hence LMA (A for *anteriore*, or front). It appeared in 1981, with a Lamborghini V12, and was to be developed as the LM 002, announced as a series-production model in Autumn 1985.

Function shaped the LMs, with only the angular wheel arches to suggest a relationship to Lamborghini's supercars. The basis was a steel tubular frame, while the bodywork was in glass-reinforced plastics (wings, bonnet and roof) or aluminium (doors). Rarely among off-roaders, LMs rode on all-independent suspension, with double wishbones and coil springs all round, and on 11-inch wide alloy wheels with special Kevlar-reinforced Pirelli tyres. They rode high, with no underbody protrusions (such as the lower part of the gearbox) exposed to off-road obstacles, and exhausts stoutly protected. Ground clearance was within fractions of an inch of being a foot (300mm) . . .

LM 002 was powered by the quad-cam 5.2 litre V12, virtually in Countach QV form, with its six Webers requiring that bonnet-top bulge that made the vehicle look even beefier. It drove through a heavy-duty 5-speed ZF gearbox, with a 2-speed transfer box to give a 10-speed transmission. Four-wheel drive was part-time, with free-wheeling front hubs, to be locked in manually for off-road use.

Left: The Cheetah was a massive vehicle, one characteristic that was carried over to the LM002 (opposite).

Left: The LM002 cockpit was fitted out luxuriously.

The body was angular, with four seats in the cabin, and two more on an open rear deck. Fittings and furnishings were to depend on the customer, for the LM 002 was offered in military and luxurious private owner forms. Some were sold to Middle East armed forces, but maintenance was not simple (or cheap), and most of these were to be sold on for civilian use, and presumably some are still bounding over dunes in areas where they first saw military use.

SPECIFICATION	LM 002
ENGINE	60 degree V12, dohc, 5167cc
HORSEPOWER	450bhp @ 6800rpm
TRANSMISSION	Manual 5-speed (high and low ranges, giving ten speeds)
CHASSIS	Multi-tubular
SUSPENSION	Independent front and rear
BRAKES	Disc front, drum rear
TOP SPEED	195km/h (121mph)
ACCELERATION	0-100km/h (62mph): 8.5 seconds

The transmission took up more cabin space than a normal tunnel, because of the high-mounted gearbox and centre differential. But within the overall width of 2000mm (78.7in) there was room for four generous and necessarily supportive seats ('dickey' passengers had simpler seats, with a nautical hand rail, and a tonneau cover was a useful accessory). High-quality leather in abundance further distanced the interior from the utilitarian exterior, and air conditioning was only to be expected. The fascia was sensible, although in an unfortunate Lamborghini tradition the arrangement of minor controls was not (the broad centre console provided a housing for some of these).

While it might have looked like a small truck from some angles, and sometimes felt like one from the high seats, the LM 002 was no mean performer. Few would have disputed the 'fastest production off-roader' claim. It would float over large bumps, in its very, very low first gear it would climb slopes at improbable angles, while mud and sand scarcely hindered its progress.

On the road it was less certain, with a tendency to wander coupled with insensitive power-assisted steering, and with brakes that were only just up to the task of arresting its 2700kg (5952lb) from high speeds. It was almost alarmingly fast: Lamborghini gave a 201km/h (125mph) top speed,

LM002 sales literature exploited images of luxury and power, including 'glove soft leather seats and interior trim' (top). But the controls were somewhat scattered. The V12 engine, however, was more accessible than in most of its car installations.

and 195km/h (121mph) was measured in independent tests. The 287 litre (63 gallon) fuel tank emptied at an astonishing rate – 20-40 litres/100km (7-14mpg) was the factory figure, 30 litres/100km (9.4mpg) was one test figure, and that did not involve dune climbing.

LM 003 was aimed at the military market, and was simplified with a proprietary 3-litre turbo diesel.

It was seriously under-powered, and did not progress beyond the one-off demonstrator stage.

LM 004, on the other hand, had the 7.2 litre Lamborghini V12 designed for power boats. Its maximum power output, 420bhp, was less than the LM 002's 450bhp, but it was delivered at lower revs and the torque figures were much better.

Lamborghini found enough customers to keep LM 002 in production until 1992, and has since revived the idea of a new off-roader, although the first proposals were set aside.

LM 002 will be difficult to follow, in terms of motoring sensations, but then Diablo succeeded Countach . . .

Below: The LM had high-speed road capability.

Lamborghini in Racing

ALMOST AS soon as Ferruccio Lamborghini's car company intentions became known, enthusiasts expected him to enter racing, and especially to challenge Ferrari on the circuits, as he intended to in the road supercar sphere. Key technical staff looked forward to racing, too, and were to quit when Lamborghini stuck firmly to his

'no-racing' policy. Importantly, product and marketing manager Ubaldo Sgarzi also opposed the manoeuvres of the racing lobby.

Development engineer Bob Wallace was allowed to build up the one-off stripped and tuned Jarama and the Jota lightweight version of the Miura, but these were not raced. His Urraco circuit

car was, just once in a minor event. He followed one-time colleagues Dallara and Stanzani, leaving when it became clear in the mid-1970s that Lamborghini was not going to set up a competitions department.

The British importer, Portman Garages, was responsible for a short-lived racing effort in 1986. The 'Lamborghini Countach QVX' for Group 1

Below: Lamborghini is proclaimed discreetly on the engine cover of a Lambo 291 in 1991.

sports-car racing comprised a Tiga GC285 developed by Spice with a Countach V12. Resources were inadequate and the car started in just one race, when Tiff Needell placed it fifth in a non-championship event at Kyalami late in the year.

A Spice-Lamborghini announced late in 1990 promised more, and with Japanese backing the intention was to contest the 1991-92 championship series. For this, Lamborghini was to produce engines to be developed and serviced by Heini Mader in Switzerland. But Spice went into receivership early in 1991, and in top-flight sports-car racing the Lamborghini V12 was seen only in a

car built by Austrian Franz Konrad, which was plagued by lack of finance and development.

Meanwhile, in 1988 Lamborghini had moved towards Formula 1. Encouraged and largely funded by Chrysler, Lamborghini Engineering was set up in a Modena factory, with long-time Ferrari engineering supremo Mauro Forghieri in charge of design, and one-time Ferrari team manager Daniele Audetto as manager.

Forghieri laid out a 3.5 litre 80 degree V12 Grand Prix engine, conventional and handsome, with 'Lamborghini' and 'Chrysler' on its cam covers. This was a serious programme.

Above: The V12 was first seen in F1 in the Lola LC89, in a modest entry into Grand Prix racing.

In 1989 'over 600bhp at 13,000rpm' was claimed, and by 1991 this had risen to 700bhp at 13,800 rpm. But this 3512 engine was never adopted by a leading team, despite strenuous efforts by Audetto. Gérard Larrousse's Lola team used it in 1989, and late in the year Philippe Alliot scored a championship point. The next year was Lamborghini's best in Formula 1, with Lola and Lotus using the engine, for sixth and eighth places respectively in the World Championship.

For 1991 Lamborghini Engineering designed its own car, funded by a Mexican who dropped out before the season started. Italian industrialist Carlo Patrucco picked up the bills, and Larrousse's team became Lambo Formula, soon associated with Patrucco's Modena Team SpA. Larini started the season with a seventh place, but after that the cars were qualified to start in only three GPs.

Venturi and Minardi used the engines in 1992, each scoring a single point, then in 1993 Larrousse ran a team under his own name. It scored three points, but there were no resources for engine development. Final efforts to place the V12 with a major team came to nothing, Chrysler support was withdrawn, and Lamborghini disappeared from GP circuits.

In 1995 a pair of factory-prepared Diablos were raced by Japanese Lamborghini Owners' Club members in a local series, achieving some good results through reliability. That can be seen as a prelude to the Philippe Charriol Super Sport Trophy series in 1996.

This was a one-model series of seven races for the Diablo SV-R, with professional and gentleman driver categories. One of the sponsors was Lease Plan – France, and the cost of outright purchase could be avoided through their leasing options, which made it possible to obtain a car and technical support package on two- or three-year plans, ' with the intention to purchase'. It was suggested that participation in the planned 1996 and 1997

Below: The legend on the engine cover records 'Chrysler powered by Lamborghini' on this 1992 Venturi. This was another lightweight GP team, which scored only one World Championship point.

Above: SV-R was the first Lamborghini produced for racing, here actually at the Goodwood Festival of Speed. Left: Gérard Larrousse was involved with several Lamborghini-powered F1 efforts, in 1993 with his own Larrousse LH93. Four years later he initiated a GT racing programme. Below left: Minardi's smart M192 used Lamborghini engines in 1992.

championships on a two-year lease could cost little more than a car, paid for outright, for the lease amounted to an extended-payment scheme.

The first race was the supporting event at Le Mans in 1996, a nine-lap (122km/76-mile) event which attracted a full field. Michel Neugarton won it at 177.92km/h (110.56mph), which compared with the 24-hour race winner's average speed of 200.60km/h (124.65mph).

Lamborghini committed to building 25 cars for each season, thereby achieving a sales boost of around 10 per cent, and at last gratifying all those enthusiasts who had always expected the marque to go racing . . .

Index